Selection
Interviewing
for
Managers

Continuing Management Education Series

Under the Advisory Editorship of Albert W. Schrader

Selection Interviewing for Managers

THOMAS L. MOFFATT
Management Dynamics, Inc.

Harper & Row, Publishers

New York   Hagerstown   Philadelphia   San Francisco   London

Senior Production Manager: Kewal K. Sharma
Compositor: Photo Graphics Inc.
Printer and Binder: The Maple Press Company
Art Studio: Vantage Art Inc.

Library of Congress Cataloging in Publication Data

Moffatt, Thomas L
  Selection interviewing for managers.

  (Continuing management education series)
  Includes index.
  1. Employment interviewing. I. Title. II. Series.
  HF5549.5.I6M64   658.31'12   78-9302
  ISBN 0-06-044573-4

Contents

Preface

As a management consultant who works with hundreds of managers, executives, and employment specialists in business, government, and educational institutions every year, I have a very definite feeling for the interview process as it is used in the selection environment. One can't be exposed to hundreds of interviews that have been conducted by everyone from the beginner who has never been involved with interviewing prior to this experience to the professional with over 20 years of experience without having some specific thoughts about the interview as a tool of selection.

On the basis of my extensive experience, I have designed this book for basic interviewers—those people who are learning to interview and who need communication techniques, an understanding of the process, and a no-nonsense system which will get them where they wish to go—and for managers and executives who occasionally are required to conduct interviews and make hiring decisions but who have little or no formal training in the interview processes. I also offer it as a refresher for the professional interviewer who wishes to update or upgrade his or her skills in today's complex world of selection and/or rejection of candidates. Another of my objectives was to write a book which could act as a basic reference for the now numerous interviewing training courses.

As interviewers become more sophisticated in their art, they will adapt the suggested techniques to their own environment and to their own special needs.

Special thanks to Linda Hilton, who was of invaluable assistance in organizing and editing the material for this book, and to Dr. Al Schrader of the University of Michigan Graduate School of Business, whose encouragement allowed me to find time from my consulting business to complete this effort.

As an employment practitioner for many years, I have a great deal of empathy for those who are face to face with a prospective applicant and told to "talk to em." I hope that this book will help to guide you through some of the difficulties faced by all beginning interviewers.

Thomas L. Moffatt

Selection
Interviewing
for
Managers

Chapter 1
Selection
Interviewing –
An Overview

What is selection interviewing? What should it be, what should it *not* be, and what problems keep it from being all that it ought to be? The interviewer who wishes to sharpen his or her interviewing skills would do well to examine these questions briefly before tackling the techniques of the interviewing process.

THE STATE OF THE ART

The basic purpose of selection, or employment, interviewing is, of course, to choose the best person to fill a specific job. This process entails the evaluation of a field of available job applicants in the context of available job openings, so that each applicant's qualifications may be compared with the job requirements. Ideally, information gathered through the interview process will be integrated with information from as many other sources as are available, in order to make this applicant–position match. These other sources may include the actual job specifications; data gathered by the company's personnel department; other interviews, in a multiple interviewing process; reference checks or letters of recommendation; and comparison with data on other persons who have performed successfully in similar jobs. But, even if an interviewer has information from all these other sources, the interview will ultimately be used as the basic selection tool, and the interviewer will want to conduct it in such a way that he or she has the greatest possible chance of making the right decision about the applicant's suitability for the job.

Unfortunately, there is no known formula for conducting an interview that will assure the interviewer of infallability in selecting the best candidate. Interviewing is not a science; we have not yet reached a level of sophistication that will allow us to gather certain predetermined data, plug it into a computer, and read the outcome with complete assurance that we are correct. Perhaps interviewing will never reach this level of technology, because of the human element involved in employment selection.

However, interviewing has progressed to the point where it can properly be called an art. An increasing number of corporations are realizing that skilled interviewers are invaluable; they are able not only to pinpoint those applicants who have the highest potential for success within the company, but also to influence these desirable applicants to join the firm. With this increasing awareness on the part of corporate executives, professionals have begun to study the interviewing process and to offer suggestions for improvement and standardization of the process. This concurrent development of awareness on the one hand and provision of the means for improvement on the other has just recently brought about vast improvement in the quality of interviewing, and the cycle shows no sign of abating.

There are, of course, weaknesses in the interview method that may never be completely overcome. Among the greatest are:

Lack of Uniformity. The nature, length, and content of the interview vary with each interviewer. This lack of uniformity can be minimized within a company through a conscious effort toward that end but cannot be eliminated entirely without sacrificing other desirable characteristics of the interview.

Lack of Objectivity. This also varies among interviewers and will probably never be completely overcome.

Failure to Recognize the Limitations of the Interview. For example, many interviewers try to pattern the interview as a test of intelligence, creativity, or reaction under stress. If these qualities are indeed valid criteria for the job in question, there are more accurate tools than the interview for their assessment.

The Time Restraints on the Interview. Many interviewers feel it is futile to try to explore all the salient aspects of the candidate's personality and background in the time allowed for the interview—especially the campus screening interview, where time schedules must be rigidly adhered to.

The Interviewer's Feeling that He or She Lacks Authority. In many—perhaps most—cases, the final hiring decision is made by someone higher up the management ladder.

Lack of Training on the Part of the Typical Interviewer. Most interviewers today fall into one of two categories: the full-time professional interviewer, or the manager or executive who has to do a little interviewing on the side. Both tend to lack training and experience in interviewing but for different reasons. The professional interviewing position is too often viewed as a training position; that is, it is assigned to a person from another area of the organization as a first step toward grooming him or her for a career opportunity in personnel. After a year or two on the job, just as the trainee may be developing some skills as an interviewer and some insight into the company's needs, he or she is promoted to another position in personnel or to a higher management position and is replaced by another inexperienced person. On the other hand, managers or executives who have to interview occasionally rarely consider interviewing to be one of their primary job functions. Thus, they are seldom inclined to actively seek ways of improving their interviewing skills. Until recently, both types of interviewers faced the additional problem of the inavailability of effective training in interviewing, even if they wanted it.

Now, the ability to select effective people is becoming a career field in many organizations, with the appropriate rewards systems and financial remunerations available to those who wish to make a professional commitment. Training courses and materials have also begun to be available; so the lack of training and experience among interviewers can be combatted—assuming companies will recognize the need to provide training for this important function. Unfortunately, some do not.

The foregoing list of weaknesses in the interviewing process is discouraging in one sense: Most of these weaknesses are inherent in the process. We can greatly reduce their adverse effects on our results through improved interviewing techniques, but we will never completely eliminate them. Still, despite these problems and limitations, the interview remains our basic employment selection tool. It can, if used effectively, be invaluable in determining the following: the technical background and competence of the applicant; the applicant's ability to fit the company, department, and other employees; whether the applicant is the type of person who will fit well and wear well; the apparent growth potential of the applicant; and the ability of the company to satisfy the goals and ambitions of the applicant.

THE VALIDITY QUESTION

Wherever interviewers gather for discussion or training, it is only a matter of time before someone asks, "How valid is the interview as a part of the selection process?"

Unfortunately, the validation of the interview as a selection tool has been retarded, so that the answer to the validity question would have been, until quite recently, "Not at all valid," or, at best, "Who knows?" And the retardation has been brought about, at least in part, by the very segments of our society whose cooperation was necessary to make interviewing a valid tool. This can probably best be illustrated by a brief anecdote.

A few years ago, the director of a leading Midwestern management training center had been asked by many businesses and organizations in the area to provide a course in interviewing. The search for help in creating such a course led to contacting the chairperson of the psychology department of a prominent Midwestern university. Would anyone from the department be available to assist in establishing a curriculum and offering instruction to meet the needs of local interviewers? The chairperson not only refused to help but was actually irate that assistance of this nature had been sought. Professionally, the chairperson knew of no studies that verified the validity of the interview as a selection tool. Therefore, no assistance could be offered in any undertaking to provide instruction of this kind.

This attitude has been all too prevalent in the academic and research worlds. Members of these communities have been reluctant to devote their efforts to a process whose validity has not been proven—at the very time when thousands of interviewers were groping for assistance in making their interviews more valid. Astute interviewers knew that the validity of the interview could never be verified until development and refinement of the process had been achieved, but they could get little or no help from the "experts" in bringing about this development and refinement. Meanwhile, hiring decisions continued to be made by untrained interviewers with virtually no input from the research and academic community. The vicious circle had been established: The interviewing process was invalid because there was no adequate training, and there was no adequate training because the process was invalid.

At last, times are changing. Techniques and instruction for interviewers are improving, and efforts are under way to show that the interview can be a valid selection tool if the trained interviewer can meet certain criteria. These validation efforts have been given impetus by Title VII and Equal Employment Opportunity (EEO) validity requirements for any tool used in the selection process. But even without the threat of legal action against discriminatory selection practices, validation studies would have been undertaken on the initiative of forward-thinking executives who realize the importance of refining the art of interviewing so that confidence may be placed in the accuracy of its results.

The cone approach to interviewing, proposed in the forthcoming chapters, is designed to simplify validation. It structures interviews in such a way that interviewers working for the same organization can be trained to run similar profiles and to establish similar objectives for various kinds of interviews at various selection levels. Current research is confirming the validity of this approach, and the actual statistics from these studies should be available in the near future. Meanwhile, preliminary results, discussions with EEO, and many recent court decisions have increased our confidence that we are on the right track with the cone approach to interviewing. If individual organizations would do some in-house studies on the criteria for their respective jobs, they could readily adapt the cone format to meet present EEO constraints and requirements, while increasing their own assurance that they are selecting the candidates with the highest potential for success in specific positions within their particular organizational framework.

The validity of the interview, then, depends upon the expertise and training of interviewers and upon the interviewing tools and techniques they utilize. A brief glimpse of some of the barriers to effective and valid selection interviewing will illustrate the need for concentrated effort to upgrade interviewing practices and procedures.

MISGUIDED APPROACHES TO INTERVIEWING

In some cases, interviews fail even before they begin, because the interviewer's approach is all wrong. For some examples of what the interview should *not* be, let's observe three common types of interviewer.

The "Application Reader"

This interviewer has probably learned how to interview by watching the boss. He usually begins the interview with a rather stilted introduction and then immediately rivets his attention on the application blank, data sheet, or resumé submitted by the candidate. He goes over each bit of information on the application with the interviewee, asking questions whose answers have already been provided on the sheet. If he deviates from the application at all, it is to ask brief questions of a factual nature: "Why did you decide to leave school before you received your degree?"; "How did you get a summer job with that organization?" When the applicant has finished answering a particular question (or, all too often, while she is still in the process of answering it), the interviewer frantically searches the application for his next question. Upon exhausting the information on the application, he tells the applicant a little about the job and the company and concludes the interview.

To an observer who has only considered the interview superficially, this may seem to be an adequate approach, and certainly a traditional one. However, analysis of the information obtained through this exercise shows that it tends to be redundant. The interviewer wastes valuable interview time in verification of the information already available in written form. Furthermore, the "application reader" tends to ask questions which elicit very brief, terse answers. Unless the candidate is a naturally gregarious person who takes command of the interview and volunteers information beyond the scope of the question, she is at a definite disadvantage. She has not been given the opportunity to present herself, her background, or her career goals in a meaningful way in relation to the available position. She has probably not even displayed much of her personality. Finally, she has no doubt developed the opinion that the interviewer is a not-very-dynamic individual, whose lack of interest-in the applicant is apparent from both his failure to study the application data beforehand and his frequent refusal to look at or listen to the applicant during the interview.

This approach, then, leaves much to be desired. It fails to provide the kind of in-depth information needed even to recommend the applicant for another interview at a later date, and it leaves the applicant feeling dissatisfied about her own participation in the interview process and her failure to establish a warm relationship with the interviewer.

The "Super Salesperson"

A hearty handshake and a rather vociferous welcome signal the beginning of an interview conducted by the "super salesperson." This species of interviewer is generally found among sales managers and in other occupations requiring a strong, out-going personality and a gift for verbalization and persuasion.

Once the "super salesperson" has greeted his applicant, he immediately begins to overpower him or her with information about the job, the company, and the products sold or the services rendered. If he does ask the applicant any questions about his or her background or goals, he may interrupt in mid-response through his eagerness to impress upon the candidate his own opinion that he represents the finest organization in the world and the only one in which the applicant could possibly find a satisfying career.

When the "super salesperson" has concluded his dissertation with more hearty handshakes and perhaps a slap on the applicant's back, he has acquired little or no information about his potential employee. The interviewer has completely overshadowed the applicant, talking perhaps 90 percent of the time while listening only 10 percent. Like the "application reader," the "super salesperson" has taken an approach that not only fails to provide information on which to base an evaluation of the applicant, but also leaves the cadidate with the feeling that he or she has been denied the opportunity to express personal strengths and goals in relation to the position. This approach is really not an assessment or selection interview at all, but a sales pitch directed at the applicant prior to determining whether he or she is even worthy of consideration for the "product"—in this case, the position with the company.

The "super salesperson," as a result of his interview, can evaluate the applicant only on the basis of looks and superficial personality traits. (Often, the "super salesperson" will recommend the candidate who shook hands most heartily and who appeared to be most interested in the sales talk about the company.)

The "Amateur Psychologist"

The "amateur psychologist" has probably taken one or two courses in basic psychology and has possibly been exposed to a book about body language. He also usually comes equipped with a memorized list of questions taken from a magazine article on the interviewing methods used by clinical psychologists or psychiatrists. Typically, he begins his interview with a series of very personal questions about the applicant's family background: his father's position in the family, his relationships with his brothers and sisters, and whether he liked his mother better than his father, for example. The "amateur psychologist" tends to include quite a few questions that are illegal today, but that doesn't seem to bother him. He may proceed from family topics to questions that probe into other interpersonal relationships: "How did you feel about your teachers?"; "Did you see your drill instructor in the Army as a father figure?" Finally, he may try to lure the applicant into summing up his own personality in a word or two by asking questions such as: "If I offered you money, status, self-satisfaction, or security, which would you choose?", or "What one word would you say describes your greatest strength?"

The "amateur psychologist" isn't satisfied merely with asking "psychological" questions during the interview. He proceeds to assign psychological or behavioral titles to the responses and reactions of the applicant and to predict total behavior patterns on the basis of these few responses. It never seems to bother the "amateur psychologist" that highly trained and experienced psychologists would hesitate, on such short exposure, even to make some of the simpler deductions which the interviewer considers as "fact." The naiveté of this approach has become a real problem in recent years, because of the rapidly growing number of untrained interviewers who believe they are demonstrating their intellectuality through their pseudopsychological approach. Hiring recommendations based on this type of interview are generally worthless, because they are based on totally unfounded conclusions about the applicant's psychological make-up. The applicant, meanwhile, may well feel resentful, or at best uncomfortable, as a result of the sensitive and personal questions he had been required to answer. He will undoubtedly leave the interview with the feeling that his privacy has been grossly invaded.

Now, at first glance, it would seem that, in criticizing these three approaches to the interview, we are really criticizing the personality of the interviewer and saying that he or she should not let it intrude into the interview situation. But this is not the case at all. Every interviewer (and every applicant, for that matter) brings to the interview situation a unique personality, including mannerisms, actions, and reactions. Otherwise, interviewing would be a very dull affair indeed. But the interviewer must also bring into the interview situation a plan that will foster the attainment of certain objectives, and that is what is missing from the three approaches we have just reviewed. In other words, the right approach is the approach that will allow the interviewer to gather the information needed in order to make an intelligent decision or recommendation regarding the applicant's suitability for the job. This is where our "application reader," "super salesperson," and "amateur psychologist" miss the mark; this is why their approaches illustrate what an interview should *not* be.

STUMBLING BLOCKS FOR UNTRAINED INTERVIEWERS

In addition to a misguided general approach to the interview, there are several reasons for the failure of untrained interviewers to make the interview an effective selection tool. Some of the most common are discussed briefly in the following paragraphs.

Absence of Viable Objectives

In discussing the three ineffectual approaches above, we touched on the subject of interview objectives. Viable objectives are essential if an interview is to accomplish its purpose. Supposedly every interviewer has some vague notion of his or her overall objectives—such as, to select the best person for the job or to assess a candidate's strengths and place them where they can be optimized—but this is not sufficient to supply structure and substance to the interview. The interviewer who has no objectives beyond these vaguely defined and all-encompassing ones will find, all too often, that he has not even approached his goal because he had no interim objectives to help him chart his course toward the ultimate objective. In other words, he can be compared to a military leader whose stated objective is to conquer the world. This objective may or may not be viable, depending on the military's resources and any number of other factors, but even if it is theoretically viable, it will never be realized unless interim objectives are set whereby the ultimate objective will be reached. The military leader might set as specific objectives, for instance, the overthrow of China, the submission of specified European nations, and the negotiation of specific treaties with African and South American nations. Upon establishing these objectives, he will set up even more specific objectives for reaching each of the intermediate goals. If a war is to be waged in China, he will want to know the objective for each separate skirmish or battle, for each platoon or division involved in that battle, and so forth. The alternative to such a set of articulated objectives would be to recruit a military force, gather its personnel together, and say to them: "Okay, guys, your mission is to conquer the world. Now go out and do it." The inefficiency, bedlam, and failure that would result is easily predictable.

The above analogy may seem oversimplified to the point of being ridiculous, yet many interviewers fail to see that they are being just as unreasonable when they set as their only objective the "conquering of the world"—in this case, the selection of the best candidate for the job. Without more specific objectives, their questions run aimlessly through the interview without gathering any real information that will help make that objective a reality, much as the soldiers in the above example run aimlessly about the globe without engaging in any concerted action that will contribute to realization of the overall goal of a world dictatorship. With only the one ultimate objective, both the interview and the global takeover suffer from a lack of planning based on specific objectives.

The interviewer, then, like the general, is destined to fail unless he decides exactly what he hopes to accomplish during a given interview. But there is another side to the coin. He must also make certain that his objectives are not so lofty that they have little or no chance of being realized. Let's return again to our power-hungry general. Suppose that he set the following specific objective: "On June 4, 500 men, armed with light artillery, will land by helicopter at Dulles Airport, march on the Capitol in Washington, D.C., and conquer the United States." This objective, if fulfilled, would certainly be of inestimable value toward realization of the ultimate objective of conquering the world. However, it is immediately apparent that this is not a viable objective. There is not one chance in a million that it can be met under the specified constraints and the existing circumstances.

This type of error is duplicated daily by interviewers who faithfully establish objectives for themselves but fail to analyze the viability of their goals. Unfortunately, many objectives, if attained, would be very valuable indeed in making a hiring decision—but attaining them in a 30- or 40-minute encounter with a total stranger is just not feasible. Construction of a complete behavioral or psychological profile, for example, is not a feasible objective in a screening interview. Yet many inexperienced or untrained interviewers continue to fall short of their ultimate objective because they are unwilling to relinquish unfeasible interim objectives they have set for themselves. Their interview time is wasted in struggling to attain an objective that was never viable, under the given circumstances, in the first place.

Inadequate Preparation for the Interview

Another common pitfall for the untrained interviewer is the lack of preparation prior to the initial confrontation with the candidate. All too often, interviewers seem to operate on the assumption that their job begins when the applicant walks in the door and consists solely of conversing with the applicant while he or she is present. This is especially true of managers and executives who interview only occasionally and whose minds are preoccupied with various other problems which they consider to be more a part of their "real" jobs, but it is also a prevalent attitude among some professional interviewers— especially those who believe their "gift of gab" will carry them through any situation that might arise during the interview.

A myriad of disasters can befall the interviewer who walks into an interview cold. First, of course, he will not have a well-articulated set of viable objectives; if he does have in mind any objectives at all, they will be general, rather than specifically tailored to the particular applicant being interviewed or to the particular position he is hoping to fill. A great deal of the interview may be wasted while the interviewer reads the candidate's application or resumé and tries to decide what questions to ask. When the time comes to evaluate the applicant and make a hiring recommendation, the interviewer may find that he has not even asked questions pertinent to the available job. He is likely to be embarrassed by questions from the applicant about the job or the benefits which he is not prepared to answer. And he is particularly apt to lose the most desirable candidates because his obvious lack of preparation implies a lack of interest in the applicant.

Some interviews, naturally, require more preparation than others. A recruiter who is conducting campus screening interviews for a large number of job openings will, understandably, be a little vague about the very specific details of these individual positions. He may not even know, at this point, precisely what jobs will be open by the time the student graduates; so his preparation in this area will be limited to a general background in the kinds of positions available with the company and the overall benefits program. He may also be unable to spend much time studying the backgrounds of the many students he will screen, since he may not see their data sheets until the morning he arrives on campus or even the moment the student enters the room for the interview. So the recruiter's preparation will be less intensive than, say, that of the manager who is conducting a hiring-decision interview with a professional who has already been screened, investigated by the personnel department, and recommended for a particular job. But in all cases, the maximum possible amount of preparation for the circumstances is essential. The interviewer who neglects it is cheating both himself and the applicant.

Poor Time Management

Many an interviewer—even those with extensive experience—has carefully established objectives for an interview session, meticulously studied all available information about the applicant and the job opening, and still discovered to her dismay that when the interview was concluded, she had not accomplished any of her objectives and had gathered little or no information on which to base an evaluation. All too often, the excuse is the same: "The time just ran out. We started talking about football (or his extracurricular school activities, or her first summer job in a drugstore, or the company), and before we knew it the time was up and the next applicant had arrived. We just never got around to talking about his last two jobs, or his career goals."

There is nothing wrong with talking with an applicant about football, or extracurricular activities, or summer jobs, or the company. In fact, covering these subjects may well constitute specific objectives of the interviewer. The problem arises when these subjects, or any other subjects, are covered to the exclusion of other topics that would contribute more valuable information to the evaluation process. This undesirable state of affairs may come about in a variety of ways. The interviewer may select a topic that will help her reach one of her several objectives and then pursue that topic in such depth that there is no time left for topics pertinent to the remaining objectives. The interviewer and applicant may exchange pleasantries at the first of the interview, find a topic of mutual interest that has little or nothing to do with the interviewer's objectives, and spend the entire interview period in idle chatter about this mutual interest. In some cases, the applicant may seize control of the interview and maneuver the discussion to topics that interest him but bear no relation to the interviewer's goals. Regardless of how this comes about, the results are the same: The objectives are unfulfilled, and insufficient information is obtained. The interviewer has not accomplished what she set out to because she did not manage her time properly during the interview.

Incidentally, interviewers have been known to place the blame for poor time utilization on the applicant. ("He started telling me about his outside interests, and he was still talking about them when the time was up. Every time I tried to change the subject, he went right back to his hobbies.") Every interviewer has encountered applicants who have tried to chart the course of the interview, and it is a difficult situation. However, the interviewer must learn to deal with this type of applicant if he is to maintain control over the interview and utilize his time efficiently. Time management and control of the interview are always the responsibility of the interviewer, not the applicant.

Ineffective Communication Skills

The best-laid plans of any interviewer count for naught if free-flowing and constructive communication patterns cannot be established with the applicant, for communication is the very heart of the interview. Without any communication at all, there would be no establishment of an interviewer–applicant relationship, no interchange of information, and thus no interview. Without *effective* communication, the interviewer-applicant relationship will lack rapport and may even disintegrate into an adversary situation; most of the information exchanged will be of a banal, surface nature; and the interview will fall far short of its objectives.

Before we proceed any farther with a discussion of communication, it should be pointed out that "communication" is not synonymous with "talking." A great many interviewers, failing to make this distinction, resist any suggestion that their communication habits may be reducing their effectiveness as an interviewer. If they are gregarious, if they do not feel bashful or ill at ease during the interview, if they are never at a loss for words and are, indeed, able to keep up a running stream of conversation throughout the session, then they fail to see any shortcomings in their communication skills.

Although these interviewers may possess the skills necessary for oration or the delivery of monologues, these do not qualify them as expert communicators in terms of the interview situation. In fact, a monologue is exactly the opposite of the optimum state of affairs in the interview—the optimum being a balance in communication which allows and encourages the applicant to tell the interviewer, freely and without fear, what the interviewer needs to know.

This balance of communication, based on rapport between the interviewer and the applicant, is a delicate state and one which requires constant nurturing on the part of the interviewer. The ease with which it can be achieved, even in the hands of a skilled interviewer, will vary greatly from candidate to candidate. But seldom, if ever, will it be achieved by the interviewer who talks too much, fails to really listen to the interviewee's answers, intimidates the applicant, or unknowingly signals lack of interest in the applicant by actions or mannerisms. These are some of the trademarks of overconfident interviewers who scoff at the suggestion that they need to brush up on their communication skills and who conduct interview after interview without ever establishing any meaningful two-way communication with applicants.

Hopefully, both the rookie interviewer and the old pro will find suggestions and explanations in this book that will help them to overcome any of the above problems that may be keeping their interviews from reaching maximum effectiveness. In addition to discussing general interviewing skills such as time management and communications, we propose in the following pages a complete system, or approach, to interviewing. We call it the *cone system.* This system has evolved as an easily mastered approach to interviewing which allows the interviewer to program his objectives into the interview and manage his time properly; it also aids him in establishing a good rapport with the applicant. Once learned, the system rapidly becomes second nature; it has worked well for those who use it, and it can be easily validated within a particular organization. However, we would be remiss if we implied that this is the only interviewing system that can work or that the cone system is so rigid that every interviewer must utilize it in exactly the same way. Instead, it is our hope that all interviewers, whether untrained or highly experienced, will discover, on their journey through this book, methods and procedures and insights that they can adapt to their own personalities and their existing repertoires of skills. The end result should be a sharpening of interviewing skills, an increase in understanding of the interviewing process, and a more effective end product, whether the interviewer adopts the cone system of interviewing wholesale, adapts it to meet his personal needs and preferences, or decides to stick with an entirely different approach.

Chapter 2
Communication
in the Interview

All of us, by training and experience, are communicators. From the earliest age, we learn to express our thoughts and wishes in words. Later in life, we become fairly adept at communicating in those ways that are most likely to elicit the desired response from others. Since the interviewing process essentially consists of communication between two people, both of whom are experienced in the art, it should follow that communication would flow smoothly and the interview would be easily and efficiently performed. Unfortunately, this is not always the case. It is all too easy in the interview situation for two supposedly "expert" senders and receivers of messages to send messages that are unintended or to fail to receive messages in the light in which they were meant. It would probably be safe to say that every interview which is less than satisfactory has fallen short because of some sort of breakdown or lack in the communication process. In this chapter, we will examine some of the specialized communication skills that can be utilized in the interview situation and explore the mechanics of establishing a relationship that will facilitate the flow of communication between interviewer and interviewee.

THE LEVEL OF COMMUNICATION

Need for Depth and Relevance

In personal communication, as compared with professional communication, information can be built up over a long period of time. In chatting idly with family or friends, for example, very few relevant communications on a particular subject may be received in the course of an hour. Because you have talked with this person many times before, however, you already have information to which these new, relevant communications may be added to increase your overall knowledge of that person. Furthermore, if there is not a specific purpose for your chat in the first place, other than the pleasure of the other individual's company, you probably will not care whether any really relevant communication took place or not.

Professional communication, on the other hand, generally lacks this extended time frame peculiar to personal communication. We talk professionally with someone for the specific purpose of obtaining or imparting a specific kind of information, and we often do this without the benefit of a backlog of information about the individual. This is the case, for instance, when a busy salesperson telephones a customer to get an order. A minimal amount of time may be spent in pleasantries, but during the bulk of the relatively brief conversation the salesperson will concentrate on finding out what the customer's needs are, determining how soon the merchandise is needed, letting the customer know what new products are available, and so forth. This concentration on obtaining or imparting specific kinds of information is also the purpose of the employment interview, when we have a very limited amount of time to find out everything we need to know about a person we have never seen.

The interview, then, might be defined as a specialized pattern of professional communication, within a limited time frame, initiated for a specific purpose. As such, it should focus on specific content areas, with elimination of extraneous material. It requires establishing a relationship in which the pattern of interaction and communication will consist almost exclusively of material that is relevant for the special purpose under consideration. This special purpose, of course, from the interviewer's point of view, is gathering the information needed to determine whether the applicant fits the job.

The interviewer's primary task, therefore, is to bring about a stream of communications consisting almost solely of relevant items or bits of information. The number of relevant items will be much larger and the number of irrelevant items much smaller than in a typical stream of personal communications of the same duration. Only when this is accomplished can we be assured that the interview has surpassed ordinary conversation in its relevance and, thus, its level of efficiency.

Relevance alone, however, is not sufficient to ensure the satisfactory outcome of the interview. Too often, interviewers, impressed with the need to concentrate exclusively on relevant information, will attempt to ensure relevance by firing a rapid series of direct questions at the applicant. These questions often seek factual information and encourage brief, terse responses. Usually, the session takes on a "question, answer, question, answer" format, resembling a verbal test. Not only does this type of interview tend to create stress and uneasiness in the applicant, but it also prohibits the establishment of in-depth communication, that is, communication at the level where it is possible for the candidate to go beyond an explanation of *what* has taken place to an explanation of *why* it has taken place and how he or she feels about it. This is the level of communication that must be reached during the interview if the interviewer is to acquire any understanding of the applicant beyond the bare facts and chronology of his or her background. Communication must be established at a depth that will enable the interviewer to gain insight into the applicants as people— their feelings about themselves and their experiences, attitudes, goals, and so forth.

It is clear, then, that the interviewer faces a demanding challenge. He or she must bear the burden of creating a climate that will encourage a free flow of communication, and this communication must be both relevant to the interview's purpose and at a sufficient depth to go beyond surface types of information. This is not always an easy task, since this level of communication must be established in a very short time with a total stranger, but it is not impossible for the interviewer who utilizes good communications techniques and who is aware of the mechanisms that can block the flow of communications.

Barriers to the Flow of Communication

The flow of relevant communications, on a meaningful level, can be impeded by a variety of barriers. These can be set up, either knowingly or unknowingly, by both the interviewer and the applicant. These barriers may crop up in any communication situation, but they are especially prevalent in the context of the interview because of the amount of stress inherent in the process. Interviewers may be under a certain amount of stress because they feel the urgency of selecting the right applicant and then making a good impression on him or her. Usually, though, the applicant feels significantly more stress. His career and his financial security are dependent upon his ability to put himself across to the interviewer in the most favorable light possible. He perceives the interviewer as the "insider," and himself as the "outsider" trying to get in. More important, he feels that the interviewer has the authority—perhaps undeserved—to make or break his career. If the applicant says the wrong thing or makes an unfavorable impression in this brief interview, it could have an adverse effect on him for the remainder of his life. It's little wonder, then, that he may feel he is under almost insurmountable stress, especially if he is very much in need of a job. Some of the barriers to in-depth communication that might occur under this stressful situation are discussed below.

Because we are "expert" communicators, we have learned patterns and habits of reacting to each other that are not intended to simplify or facilitate the communication process. These strategies may be designed by the applicant to protect himself against making undesirable revelations or admissions. In other words, the applicant fails to communicate properly on purpose, to avoid appearing in an unfavorable light.

Defensiveness also impedes free communication. If an applicant feels, correctly or incorrectly, that he is being criticized or attacked by the interviewer, he will counter or defend himself by resisting this attack. Not only will he resist offering the specific information which would prove the interviewer correct, but he may feel compelled to go a step farther by stretching the truth in order to prove the interviewer wrong. This defense mechanism, once activated, tends to carry over to future topics as well. The result is that many applicants, once they become defensive, continue in a pattern of resistance that impedes in-depth communication.

Often, communication is also hampered because we hear what we expect to hear, rather than what is actually being said. Experience has taught us to anticipate what we will hear next. We listen only for what fits our purposes, or until we have "classified" the speaker or his or her remarks in our mind. Probably ineffective listening habits have destroyed the flow of communication in interviews more often than any other single error. If poor listening causes a question to be answered incorrectly or the answer to be misinterpreted, the entire complexion of the remainder of the interview can be changed without either participant's realizing what has occurred.

Another listening-related barrier is the listener's investment of emotion and time in the evaluation of the speaker's motives and the adaptability of the message to the listener's needs. Both parties to communication are continually coding and classifying—evaluating, sorting, accepting or rejecting, and assimilating messages. Some of this evaluation process, of course, is essential to good listening, but if the listener invests a great deal of emotion in the process, then the flow of communication can be impaired.

Often, the opinions communicated by one person will be influenced by signals that have been picked up from the other communicator. For instance, if an applicant perceives an approving attitude, he or she will tend to repeat and overemphasize the kinds of statements that brought about that approval and avoid expressing feelings that might conflict with it.

Sometimes information may be withheld because of forgetting. This may be genuine forgetting, or it may be "selective forgetting"— the tendency to forget or repress certain things because they are unpleasant to remember. In the same vein, a person may withhold or distort information not because she wants to, but simply because she is psychologically unable to produce it. For example, the applicant may be totally unable to say that a particular job is desirable because the salary will allow the family to "keep up with the Joneses." The applicant has not forgotten this, knows it is true, and wants to be truthful but is unable to make the statement because she is psychologically unprepared to admit that this is her real feeling.

Language difficulties also impede communications. The words that are chosen by one communicator must have the same meaning to the other, or communication will be faulty. In many interviews, communication lines have been tenuous because the interviewer's vocabulary was over the head of the candidate or because words with emotional connotations were interpreted differently by sender and receiver.

Although we have emphasized here the barriers to communication that may arise as a result of the applicant's stress, we would be remiss if we implied that the candidate erects all the barriers in the interview. The interviewer is under the same motivational forces which inhibit or facilitate communications or which yield distortions. To minimize these barriers, the interview must become a process in which the forces to distort or withhold communications have been eliminated or reduced to the greatest possible extent. This responsibility falls upon the interviewer. He must try to understand his own psychological make-up and that of the applicant, do his best to relieve the pressures and stress that create barriers, and formulate his remarks so that they take into account any language limitations or sensitivities of the applicant. Ultimately, the interviewer bears the responsibility for the pattern of interaction that occurs during the interview. In the remainder of this chapter, we will discuss some of the techniques that can be utilized in establishing and maintaining a rewarding relationship between the two parties involved.

VERBAL COMMUNICATION

Language and Vocabulary

Because of the symbolic nature of language it is often a poor substitute for the realities which it attempts to represent. The words we use tend to breed oversimplification and overgeneralization, so that two persons who are using the same words may in fact be using them to express entirely different ideas. On the other hand, two persons who feel the same way about a particular subject may never realize the similarity because they are using different words to describe their feeling. The difficulty of interpretation of another's comments increases as the subjective or emotional content of his or her language increases. This cannot be avoided altogether, but the skilled interviewer can attempt to use language precisely in order to minimize confusion on the applicant's part. The interviewer can also be alert to those words used by the applicant which might have more than one connotation and probe more deeply to discover exactly what the applicant means. The techniques for probing into attitudes and feelings will be discussed later, when we examine the cone system of interviewing.

The interviewer should also try to avoid using words or phrases that might have a very strong emotional connotation for the candidate—words, for instance, that might make the applicant feel particularly sensitive or defensive, such as "fired," "poor record," "quit (school)," "flunk," "welfare," "ghetto," and so forth. Of course, the amount of emotional meaning or sensitivity connected with a particular word will vary from candidate to candidate, depending upon the meaning and experiences that each associates with the word. Obviously, some of the examples just cited would have no emotional connotation at all for certain candidates, while they would have a great deal for others. If an interviewer uses a word or phrase that appears to elicit defensiveness or any type of emotional reaction from the candidate, he or she should rephrase the question or comment, using a less emotional word.

As we mentioned earlier, language difficulties can also develop simply because one communicator uses words that are unfamiliar to the other. This can often come about because the vocabulary of the interviewer exceeds that of the interviewee. Recently, an experienced interviewer talked with a young man who had a tenth-grade education, although she was more accustomed to interviewing professional-level candidates. She would notice each time she asked a question that a puzzled, uncomprehensive look came across the applicant's face, and he would fail to respond. After having to restate two or three questions, she realized that she would have to word her queries much more specifically and simplify the level of her vocabulary. As soon as she had adjusted to the applicant's level of vocabulary, she and the candidate began to understand one another, and the interview proceeded smoothly.

Since communication can only take place at the level of shared vocabulary, the interviewer whose vocabulary is extensive must take care to avoid the more difficult or exotic words with which the applicant may be unfamiliar. Even with candidates who have completed their higher education, it is sometimes necessary to rephrase questions, using a simpler vocabulary level.

Another area that frequently causes vocabulary problems is the use of in-house vernacular on the part of the interviewer. This was illustrated during a recent chat with several college students, just after they were interviewed by a representative of a large energy firm. When asked how the interviews went, all the candidates had the same comment: "We felt fine until the interviewer kept referring to our 'Q.R.'s,' and then we felt left out. We didn't know what a Q.R. was." As it turned out, the Q.R. was this particular company's terminology for the student's qualification record.

Such use of in-house slang or abbreviations not only makes the applicant feel like an outsider—as if he is not quite "with it"—but also leads to misunderstandings if the applicant interprets the word or phrase incorrectly. Of course, a chemist who is interviewing another chemist may use chemical terms, as long as he is sure they are universally used, rather than idiosyncratic terms peculiar to his own laboratory or specialty area. But the same chemist, while interviewing a secretarial candidate, would have to be more careful to avoid the casual use of chemical terminology. The same terms which were easily understood by his fellow chemist, and which probably made him feel comfortable with him, could confuse laypeople and make them feel alienated from both the interviewer and the potential job.

Although it is important to avoid talking at a level beyond the candidate's comprehension, it is equally important to avoid talking down to the candidate or patronizing him or her. A few interviewers make the mistake of assuming that job applicants are either uneducated or slightly simple-minded, especially if they are very young or are applying for a position several rungs below that held by the interviewer. Applicants usually resent the interviewer's obvious use of oversimplified or condescending language. Such usage implies that they are considered too stupid or immature to engage in normal conversation. When in doubt about an applicant's vocabulary level, the interviewer should use his or her normal vocabulary at the beginning of the interview and make modifications, if necessary, when they are indicated. Generally, it is safe to assume that the applicant can understand the words you are using unless he appears to be puzzled or his responses indicate that he has misunderstood.

Sensitive Content

The timing in verbal communication can be very important. Questions or comments that the applicant may take in stride at one point in the interview may be entirely inappropriate at another point. Especially in the early stages of the interview, when the interviewer is still trying to establish a climate conducive to in-depth communication, emotional barriers can be created by the exploration of a subject that the applicant is sensitive about or that he considers too personal to be discussed with someone he has just met. If the interviewer attempts to explore at a great depth a sensitive subject before the applicant is ready to open up, stress and resistance set in, and the flow of communication may be adversely affected for the remainder of the interview. For this reason, we usually try to start out the interview by inquiring into subjects that the interviewee is most likely to be interested in and proud of, as opposed to extremely sensitive or personal areas or areas in which the applicant has experienced dubious success. Later on, after the candidate has come to feel comfortable with the interviewer, it is often possible to discuss these kinds of subjects in depth with a minimum of discomfort or resistance on the candidate's part.

Sometimes it is the way in which questions are asked rather than their content per se which creates emotional barriers to communication. Later on, in the chapter entitled "The Cone System of Interviewing," we will discuss question focus and explore the differences between open-focus, moderate-focus, and closed-focus or direct questions. We should point out here, however, that communication barriers can quickly be erected by questions that are of improper focus. Usually, questions that are too direct are most apt to create barriers such as defensiveness or resistance, because they are perceived by the applicant as derrogatory or interrogative or because they put her on the spot for a particular answer which she may be unwilling to provide.

Most questions that are too direct or too sensitive can easily be opened up or softened up if they are worded differently. The idea here is to ask the question you want to ask, but to word it in such a way that you minimize its chance of being perceived as too personal, challenging, or threatening. Table 2.1 contains a few examples of such questions and their alternatives—questions that are too direct or sensitive on the left and the same question worded in a less offensive manner on the right. These are not intended to be a list of questions that should be asked in each interview; they merely exemplify the ways in which questions can be asked with different wording, or with a different question focus, to decrease the chance of creating emotional barriers.

We could go on and on with examples similar to those in the table, but these should be sufficient to show how the tone of the question can be moderated and made more cordial by making a slight alteration in the wording or in the question focus. There are a few rules of thumb to keep in mind here. First, avoid asking direct, point-blank questions in sensitive areas if at all possible. (Example: "Why was your sales record so poor?") In most cases, such a question will create defensiveness and destroy communication, or the candidate will already have some kind of answer for the question which may not be completely authentic. Second, if you intend to ask an applicant for negative feelings, such as her problems or dislikes on the job, ask for the positive aspects first. Along this same line, utilize a little "stroking" before posing the question. Stroking is the offering of positive feedback or compliments to the applicant before posing the sensitive question. (Example: "You must have worked very hard to handle two part-time jobs while you took a full course load. How do you think this heavy schedule affected your grades?")

Finally, be sure that questions are not asked in a challenging or threatening tone of voice. The entire tone of the inquiry can be altered, even though the actual words may be identical, when the

Table 2.1 SENSITIVE QUESTIONS AND THEIR ALTERNATIVES

TOO DIRECT OR SENSITIVE	LESS DIRECT OR SENSITIVE
Why were you fired from your last job? *or* Why are you looking for another job?	What are some of your reasons for considering other employment at this time?
Did you have trouble with your boss?	How would you describe your boss?
Why did you leave school before you got your degree?	Was there any particular reason that you decided to leave school when you did?
To what do you attribute your poor employment record?	I see you have changed jobs several times. What were some of your reasons for seeking new opportunities? *or* Everyone has problems with some aspects of their jobs. Could you describe some of the things that posed problems for you on previous jobs?
Did you get along with your co-workers?	Could you describe your relationship with a co-worker or colleague whom you were particularly close to?
What didn't you like about your last job?	Most situations have some aspects that are not as pleasant as others. Were there any less pleasant aspects of your last job?
Are you free to move?	How would you feel about moving to another city at the present time? *or* If you were relocated to another area, what problems would this present for you? (*Note:* The relocation question usually takes more time and should not be approached so directly. The whole topic can become a separate area of nondirective inquiry. See the chapter on the cone system if it is important to the interview.)
Your sales record must have been poor last year, since you didn't get a bonus.	How would you describe your sales success during the past year? *or*

Table 2.1 (*Continued*)

TOO DIRECT OR SENSITIVE	LESS DIRECT OR SENSITIVE
	We all realize that sales often reflect various conditions of the economy. Could you comment on some factors that might have precluded your meeting last year's quotas?
You mean to say you're unemployed?	At present you're not employed, then, is that correct?
I suppose you're on unemployment, huh?	Were you eligible to receive unemployment compensation after you were laid off?
Why would you think you are qualified to go into research and development, with your background?	Would you comment on how you feel you could use your background in our research and development area?

interviewer's tone of voice implies that he or she is challenging the candidate. Consider, for instance, this question: "With your background, what was your thinking when you decided to go into marketing?" Depending on the tone and inflection, the placement of stress and emphasis, this question could be a simple inquiry expressing genuine interest in the applicant's thoughts, or it could be extremely sarcastic and insulting.

NONVERBAL COMMUNICATION

Most interviewers, when they consider the importance of communication in the interview, reflect only on the verbal aspects of communication and the problems that language usage may entail. They disregard an equally important mode of communication—the nonverbal mode. Yet quite often what is communicated nonverbally has a greater impact on the outcome of the interview than does what is communicated verbally.

When inexperienced interviewers first view a videotaped replay of themselves in an interview session, they are generally taken aback by their own nonverbal behavior. They discover that they are not the way they have pictured themselves, as far as nonverbal communication is concerned. Their facial expression lines, body movements, and distracting habits appear foreign to them; some actually cannot believe that they look and act in the manner captured on the tape, although the evidence is irrefutable. After evaluating their own performance, it becomes obvious to them that they are doing things in the interview, quite apart from the words they use, which are less than effective in enhancing their ability to communicate with an applicant.

Generally, although the interviewer is oblivious to the nonverbal clues he may be sending to the applicant, the applicant is very much aware of them, even though he may not be able to describe them in so many words. If the interviewer's expressions and movements convey the message "I'm bored" or "I disapprove of you," the candidate will pick up these clues and react to them, even if the interviewer's verbal behavior is contradictory.

Eye Contact

One of the most important aspects of nonverbal behavior in the interview is the establishment of eye contact with the candidate. The interviewer can greatly enhance the willingness of the candidate to communicate freely simply by looking directly at him or her as if the subject under discussion is of interest to the interviewer. This is one reason note-taking during the interview is discouraged. Each time the interviewer looks down at his paper to take notes, he will destroy eye contact with the applicant. The overuse of the application blank during the interview will also interfere with eye contact. Many interviewers, in fact, use the application blank as a crutch, because it gives them something to look at while the applicant is talking. This, of course, is a mistake and can only hinder the communication process. A good rule for the interviewer who has trouble establishing eye contact is to remove, insofar as possible, all temptations to look elsewhere. This means eliminating note-taking entirely, leaving the application blank or other data where it is inaccessible, and perhaps putting the interviewer's back to the window to remove the temptation to gaze outside while the applicant is trying to communicate. The more distractions the interviewer removes, the greater the probability that he will establish eye contact with the applicant simply because he has nothing else interesting to look at.

It is possible to carry eye contact too far, although the vast majority of interviewers err on the side of too little rather than too much contact. Once in a while, though, an interviewer who is a very intense person will establish too much eye contact, so that he or she seems to be staring at the applicant. In such cases, the applicant may feel that the interviewer's eyes are "boring holes through him," and begin to feel extremely uncomfortable because of the intensity of the eye fixation. This, of course, also blocks the free flow of communication. An interviewer who feels that candidates are frequently uncomfortable during his or her interviews should consider this as a possible cause. Extremely intense interviewers sometimes find they have to moderate their eye contact by forcing themselves to shift their gaze away from the applicant's eyes or to change facial expressions from time to time. It should be stressed, however, that the average inexperienced interviewer most likely has the opposite problem and should be concentrating on looking at the candidate more rather than less frequently during the communication process. The trick is to look directly at the candidate, with an accompanying thoughtful or pleasant facial expression, so that the overall picture is o. ʾmeone who is listening with real interest and understanding.

Body Movements

Body language is also important during the interview. Interviewers who sit too stiffly during the entire session may communicate an air of formality that makes the applicant feel uncomfortable and inhibited. Interviewers who look more informal and comfortable, without appearing sloppy, invite freer communication. Candidates may also feel uncomfortable if the interviewer leans too far forward, because this may be perceived as a threatening posture or an attempt to become too personal—too "close" to the candidate—before the candidate is ready for this degree of proximity. Frowning or scowling, of course, can also be threatening. Some interviewers are surprised to learn that they frequently scowl when they are trying to concentrate on the applicant's meaning. In the applicant's eyes, however, the scowl may be interpreted as a sign of disapproval rather than of concentration.

Some actions have come to have definite interpretations in the minds of most observers. These interpretations may be made unconsciously, just as the gesture itself may be unconscious, but their effect on the flow of communication is unmistakable. Some such actions, both desirable and undesirable, are listed below with their interpretations.

Action	Common Interpretation
Offering a cigarette	"Relax."
Leaning back in chair	"I have plenty of time to listen."
Glancing at watch, clock, or door	"Hurry," or "I'm getting bored."
Nodding head	"I agree," or "I understand."

Silence	"I'm contemplating what you've told me."
Putting notes aside	"This is off the record."
Snapping book shut or suddenly folding up application blank	"Let's bring this thing to a close."

No doubt you can think of many other examples. The interviewer should try to avoid those with an undesirable or negative interpretation and increase his awareness of his usage of the more positive actions.

Note-taking during the interview, in addition to destroying eye contact, can be perceived as a nonverbal threat to the applicant, who is more likely to be wary of what is said if he knows it is being recorded. If the interviewer feels it is imperative to take notes, he should begin by recording something positive about the applicant rather than something negative. Too many note-takers sit with a blank sheet of paper until the applicant first admits a fault or shortcoming and then scramble to write it down. The applicant immediately jumps to the conclusion that the interviewer's notes will consist solely of derrogatory comments, and silently vows to communicate as little as possible so that the interviewer has nothing to write. This feeling is greatly reduced if the interviewer has already written down several positive comments about the applicant before a negative aspect of his background comes up. Another trick is to wait a few moments before writing down any negative comment, so that it is less apparent to the applicant that one of his weaknesses has been committed to paper. However, this advice about how to take notes is offered only because we know some interviewers will continue to take notes, regardless of exhortations to discontinue the practice. The best advice about note-taking is: Don't!

Little irritating habits on the part of the interviewer can severely disrupt the flow of communication, especially if these habits are repeated at frequent intervals. Most interviewers are completely unaware of such habits, but the applicant quickly notices them and either interprets them as signs of the interviewer's boredom or becomes so fascinated with them that his or her train of thought is lost. In either case, the communication process suffers. Distracting habits that fall in this category often include playing with a pen, pencil, or some other object on the desk; shuffling papers; drumming fingers on the table top; scratching or rubbing the head, ear, or chin; playing with the hair or beard; popping knuckles; excessive nodding of the head; or any other type of behavior that would fall into the general categories of nervous movements or "fiddling around." In one recent instance, communication was completely destroyed when the interviewer spent the entire session engrossed in his pipe. He alternately filled it, tamped the tobacco down, attempted repeatedly to light it, then scraped out the tobacco and began again. His preoccupation with this process kept him from hearing much of what the applicant was telling him; even worse, it clearly conveyed to the applicant a complete lack of interest on the interviewer's part. While some such habits are merely annoying or distracting, others can be interpreted as actual rudeness. All should be avoided.

The Setting as Nonverbal Communication

The physical setting of the interview also communicates something to the applicant nonverbally. Clean, pleasant, and quiet surroundings make the applicant feel more like communicating than do dreary, disorderly, noisy settings. Increasingly, we are encouraging the interviewer to get out from behind the desk—perhaps by arranging two chairs and a small table in one corner of the room—so that the applicant and interviewer are not separated by a barrier. This type of arrangement more nearly resembles the usual setting for intimate conversation and prevents the applicant from feeling intimidated by being on the "wrong" side of the desk. Candidates often feel timid or inferior, and thus disinclined to communicate openly, if the interviewer utilizes "status symbols" that are denied to the applicant—if the interviewer sits in a much larger or higher chair, for instance, or drinks coffee from a ceramic mug while offering the applicant a disposable plastic cup. Any arrangements that can be made to establish the equality of the two participants will increase the chances of establishing a free, open relationship that will facilitate in-depth communication.

Nonverbal Behavior of the Candidate

So far, we have focused our discussion on the nonverbal behavior of the interviewer and its effect on communication. The astute interviewer can also learn a great deal from the nonverbal behavior of the candidate, who is also constantly communicating without using spoken language. For instance, an applicant who is not yet relaxed or comfortable enough to communicate freely may show signs of anxiety such as excessive perspiration, cowering posture, halting speech or high voice pitch, rapid eye movements, drumming of fingers, clenching of fists, or failure to establish eye contact with the interviewer.

An applicant who is exhibiting these nonverbal clues at the beginning of the interview probably will not respond freely and needs to be "warmed up" more before any sensitive questioning begins. If these signs appear suddenly at a later stage of the session in an applicant who has appeared relaxed during the earlier stages, the interviewer can usually assume that he has created a situation which is threatening to the candidate, that he has induced too much stress, that he has initiated inquiry into a topic which is extremely sensitive for this particular candidate, or simply that he is dealing with a supersensitive person who must be handled with extreme care and understanding. These are signs that the interviewer should back off, take it easy on the candidate, and perhaps switch his line of questioning or soften the directness of his questions.

THE ART OF LISTENING

In discussing many of the forms of nonverbal communication in the preceding section, we touched on their relationship to the interviewer's listening habits. Some types of nonverbal behavior actually impair or facilitate the interviewer's ability to listen effectively; others convey to the candidate the impression, correct or incorrect, that the interviewer is either listening or not listening.

Of course, the act of listening per se is a nonverbal behavior—perhaps the most important type of behavior that the interviewer engages in during the interview. Yet, strangely enough, few novice interviewers are concerned about whether they will listen properly. They are most often concerned about what they will say during the interview, rather than what they will hear.

Nevertheless, faulty listening habits create many of the most common communication problems in interviewing. To illustrate one widespread problem, let's observe an interviewing workshop recently held on the campus of a large Midwestern university.

Tim Jones was completing an interview with a secretarial applicant. The instructor, who was acting as an observer, suspected that there was a breakdown in the communication relationship when he noticed that Tim was failing to follow up on some of the clues the candidate was giving him concerning deficiencies in his employment record. Following the interview, the instructor questioned Tim about some of the statements the candidate had made. Tim was most embarrassed to find that he could not remember his replies to his questions. He soon realized that he had concentrated so intently on structuring the next question that he hadn't listened to the applicant.

As Tim learned, the professional interviewer has to train himself or herself to listen. Since the average person speaks at the rate of 100–125 words a minute and we can think at about four times that rate, we soon become bored, and our minds wander. Or, as in Tim's case, we preoccupy ourselves with the next question.

Of all the techniques and skills needed by interviewers, the most difficult one to learn is that of listening. The reason lies in our prior experience and behavior. Throughout our lives, we have developed improper listening habits. When we become bored with conversation, we simply turn off our "listening apparatus" and revert to more interesting thoughts, much as we might ignore a television commercial even though the volume of the set is quite high. Gradually, we have even learned to tune out someone who is talking to us, while maintaining an interested expression and perhaps even nodding or murmuring in agreement now and then to give the impression that we are fascinated with the conversation. We have become experts at the art of not listening while appearing to listen.

Perhaps we don't miss much this way in a normal stream of personal conversation, where relevant communications are few and far between. But in an interview situation, where the goal is for nearly all communications to be relevant, we can't afford to miss even a single comment. The competent interviewer must train himself or herself to listen and to try to understand the meaning behind everything the speaker is saying. When we reach this point, we have come a long way toward the mastery of interviewing's major stumbling block.

First, let's define "listening." Listening is far more than just allowing the other person to speak. It is more, too, than a one-way process where the response is taken in but not acted upon. Real listening is neither a passive nor a permissive function but an active function in which the response to a question is taken in, thoughtfully considered, and, if appropriate, woven into the fabric of the remainder of the conversation. The good listener will listen with understanding; he will strive to learn about the other person, to be an active participant in the conversation, and to attain at least temporary unconcern with himself. In doing so, he will listen intensely enough to be able to discern what the speaker actually means, rather than accept the words he or she utters at face value. This means listening for inflections, words that could serve as clues to hidden meanings, words that could have double meanings, and things that may be left unsaid as well as those that are stated. It means following up through the use of probing techniques to discover what the speaker really thinks or feels or intends to communicate, rather than assuming that he knows what the candidate means. We will discuss these probing techniques in later chapters.

It is virtually impossible to talk and listen at the same time. Since the average untrained interviewer talks for about 75 percent of the interview, it's little wonder that he has trouble listening effectively. To avoid this common error, interviewers must learn techniques for encouraging the applicant to talk in addition to learning techniques that will improve their own listening habits.

Techniques for Better Listening

There are various levels of listening, just as there are various levels of communicating. At the most superficial depth, of course, listening involves hearing what the other person says in the literal sense. Too many interviewers fail to achieve even this surface level of listening. The interviewer must learn to listen to every word the applicant utters. This means learning to tune out distractions, such as peripheral sounds or views, so that attention is concentrated on the candidate. It also requires that interviewers give up the pretense of looking directly at the candidate while tuning him or her out. After all, it is not only for the sake of politeness that we advocate listening to the candidate—it is to the interviewer's advantage to hear everything he or she says.

Like Tim in our previous example, interviewers often fail to listen because they are thinking ahead to their next questions and trying to formulate these in their minds. Many interviewers are guilty of this because they get caught in what we call the "half-response syndrome." Here, the interviewer asks a question and listens intently to only the first half of the response before turning her thoughts elsewhere and blocking out the remainder of the response. This is just as dangerous as not listening at all. Studies have shown that the average applicant will begin his response by saying something rather banal or noncommittal; he is using the first few moments to get his thoughts together. The real meat of his reply will follow in the second half of the response, after the interviewer has already stopped listening. (Some enterprising reader will no doubt ask, "Well, why don't we just listen to the last half of every response, then, and ignore the first half?" This is equally dangerous, because quick-thinking applicants may give you the most significant part of their response first and follow it with elaboration of inconsequential data. So the only solution is to listen at all times. There will be plenty of time to formulate your next question after the candidate has concluded his response. A slight pause while you are digesting what he says and structuring your next question will not be upsetting to the candidate and in fact may be beneficial in preventing the interview from becoming a rapid-fire interrogative session.)

Sometimes, interviewers lose track of what the applicant is saying because they get so engrossed in writing down individual parts of the response that they miss the overall trend of what is said. And once in a while, even if the interviewer is trying to listen intently, the applicant's statements become so intricately involved or so confusing that it is difficult to take in his meaning. When this happens, the interviewer should review the applicant's statements to be sure she has understood correctly. For that matter, a periodic review of the statements that have just been made is a good idea even if the interviewer believes she knows exactly what the applicant intended to communicate.

So far, we have been talking about listening habits on the most superficial level. These techniques are elementary and necessary, but they don't go far enough for a situation, such as the interview, where in-depth listening is required. In this case, the listener must not only hear all the words that are said but must go beyond them to discern their real meaning. As the interviewer, don't concentrate solely on facts; listen for "between-the-lines" meaning and for attitudes that the applicant may be conveying. Listen carefully for verbal clues that will give you insight into the applicant's attitude and personality. These clues may include the tone and projection of his voice; his enunciation; his word selection and sentence structure; word pictures that may threaten physical force; or any other clues to his general mental set. Gradually develop the habit of listening for difficult hidden situations or clues to areas of sensitivity. Listen for what is purposely omitted as well as for what is included in the response. Weigh and evaluate the points the interviewee is presenting and think ahead to where he may be leading, without getting so involved in this mental exercise that you lose track of his current trend of thought. Be alert for emotion-laden words which the adept applicant may throw in to color the facts. And finally, be aware of your own deep-seated prejudices and biases, which may affect what you think you hear. These will be discussed more fully in the next chapter.

Once the candidate has completed his response, the interviewer must digest and evaluate what she has heard to be sure that her original question was answered satisfactorily and completely. Some interviewers will become so engrossed in what the candidate has said that they fail to realize he or she has talked all around the edges of the subject without ever actually addressing the question. Sometimes this is accidental, but often it is purposeful. To detect this, the interviewer must utilize "dual listening"—a technique that involves comparing the response to the question in order to discern whether the requirements of the question were met and then rephrasing the question or probing further if necessary. This is particularly necessary when interviewing the verbally adept, overly talkative candidate.

In-depth listening, then, requires not only hearing what the candidate says, but also discerning how he feels and why he feels that way. Listening on this level is not always easy, especially if the candidate is uninteresting or if he has little verbal facility, but it is absolutely essential to the interviewer who wants to meet her objective of determining whether a particular candidate is suited for a particular job. As we get into discussions of the cone system of interviewing and the probing techniques that accompany it, we will see that proper listening skills are vital to the operation of the system.

Chapter 3
The Interviewer —
Understanding
and Improving
Himself or Herself

Interviewers are often concerned about their ability to understand the applicants they interview—and with good reason—since this is an important factor in effective communication and accurate evaluation. But too often these same interviewers are unconcerned with their own understanding of themselves. This is where understanding must start.

THE INTERVIEWER AS AN INDIVIDUAL

Interviewers can never hope to understand the *other* individual perfectly, because the nature of their jobs requires them to deal with many different candidates, each for only a very brief time. But they can greatly increase their ability to understand these candidates by first increasing their understanding of themselves. The mature interviewer should pose these questions and strive to answer them as honestly as possible: What factors in my personality or in my background influence the ways in which I treat various types of candidates? What personality factors cause me to react to one candidate in a particular way, while reacting to another candidate in a totally different manner? What variables within *me* influence the way in which I form my opinions of others, or interpret what they say, or evaluate their abilities? What situations do I create in the interview, as a result of my own characteristics, that detract from the effectiveness of the interview? What can I do to handle my feelings in a more mature manner and to improve my effectiveness as an interviewer? What interviewing skills and techniques do I need to brush up on, in order to communicate with and evaluate candidates more accurately?

Of course, no interviewer can answer these questions on a one-time basis and then rest assured that his or her self-understanding is complete. Most people, in fact, do not even recognize many of the attitudes, traits, and feelings within themselves that greatly affect their actions and their reactions to others. The mature, effective interviewer must enter into an ongoing self-appraisal, beginning with the understanding that he or she is an individual, continuing through a perpetual introspective study of his or her own feelings and motives, and hopefully culminating in the development of enough maturity and self-understanding to compensate for those individual traits that detract from his or her effectiveness as an interviewer.

Biases and Prejudices

Most of us would like to think, or at least to convince others, that we have no prejudices. In recent years, "prejudice" has come to have very negative connotations, associated primarily with Anglo-Saxons who express suspicion or dislike of minority-group members. But this is just one definition of prejudice, although a very important one. Prejudice, according to one leading dictionary, can also entail "an adverse judgment or opinion formed beforehand without knowledge or examination of the facts" or "a preconceived preference or idea; bias." A bias, similarly, is defined as "preference or inclination that inhibits impartial judgment."

Attitudes or opinions that fit any of these definitions of "bias" or "prejudice," then, clearly hinder the processes of objective communication and evaluation during the interview, and all of us have them. We have acquired them through the myriad of experiences and the unique backgrounds that make us individuals. It is highly unlikely that we are ever going to be rid of them, but we can go a long way toward conquering their undesirable effects if we acknowledge them, attempt to understand them, and learn to compensate for them.

There are a number of ways in which the interviewer's biases and prejudices work to interfere with objective evaluation of the candidate. There are, of course, the obvious prejudices against minority candidates and women on the part of some interviewers. Although the government has legislated against discriminatory *practices* in interviewing minorities and women, it cannot, unfortunately, enforce legislation that will prevent discriminatory *thoughts*. These prejudicial attitudes, even at the subconscious level, can cause an interviewer to seriously underevaluate an applicant because he or she is unable to see the applicant's good points or to believe those good points really exist.

In recent years, the "liberated woman" has been the victim of a good many biased evaluations. Older male interviewers, especially, tend to be suspicious of the "women's libber" rhetoric, with the result that they seldom evaluate such applicants favorably. Based on the interviewer's feelings that his organization isn't ready for the liberated woman or that he himself believes women should be less aggressive or ambitious, he fails to evaluate her qualifications and skills objectively.

Quite a few nonminority interviewers (that is, white, Anglo-Saxon males) who are interviewing minorities for professional-level jobs are hampered by their prejudices in evaluating these candidates. These interviewers often feel that white males would be better qualified for the higher-level jobs, and they resent the fact that they are required to make an effort to hire minorities. As a result, they go out of their way to find excuses to eliminate the minority candidates from consideration. In many cases, these actions are unconscious; the biases and prejudices are so deep-seated that, unless the interviewer is carefully trained in self-evaluation, he will continue to believe that he has been entirely objective in deciding that the minority candidate is unqualified for the position. This type of interviewer is no doubt screening out some very good candidates for the wrong reasons, as well as exposing the company to discrimination suits. Interviewers who represent the majority class and who are in a position to interview members of minority groups must be very careful not to let their biases and prejudices surface to interfere with valid assessment of these candidates.

Sometimes our biases and prejudices are not strong enough to cause outright rejection, but are sufficient to cause us to feel uncomfortable with persons who are different from ourselves. We believe we cannot communicate with these persons because we feel unable to understand them. Many interviewers feel uncomfortable if the applicant is very much older or very much younger than they are. Many blacks feel uncomfortable interviewing whites, and vice versa. Women who are accustomed to interviewing women and men who are accustomed to interviewing men may feel uncomfortable when faced with an applicant of the opposite sex. In most of these cases, the "real" differences between interviewer and candidate are insignificant, compared with the differences interviewers imagine because of their biases and prejudices. The mature, experienced interviewer must learn how to handle and relate to each type of person effectively and comfortably through associating with a variety of people and through attempting to understand their feelings and motives as individuals, rather than as representatives of a particular group or class.

Nearly everyone is also simply turned off or turned on by particular types of persons. Even in cases where the interviewer himself does not recognize this bias, his preferences can cause him to lose objectivity in evaluating the candidate. For example, certain individuals are partial to well-dressed, handsome, articulate individuals. If an interviewer with this bias is confronted with a particularly nice-looking candidate, he may be so impressed that he fails to recognize the candidate's obvious faults in other areas. Another candidate who is much better qualified for the job may turn off the interviewer because of his poor appearance or informal dress. In other words, the interviewer, because of his bias, never gets beyond the surface of the candidates. Through experience and introspection, the interviewer must understand himself or herself and guard against these hasty and ill-founded evaluations, realizing that judgment can be affected by irrelevant factors that cause the interviewer to be turned off or turned on.

Another place where biases can creep in is the evaluation of someone who is already known to the interviewer—perhaps someone already employed within the company who wants to change departments or who is seeking a promotion. These people are hard to evaluate, precisely because we already know something about them. Our prejudices and biases may be working overtime. Perhaps this applicant has had a poor record to date, because the job he held didn't suit his background and skills very well. He is now applying for a transfer to a job for which he is better suited, but the interviewer will tend to see him as a poor choice on the basis of negative comments he has heard. On the other hand, a very similar applicant from outside the organization might tend to look more attractive because the interviewer doesn't know as much about him. References or previous employer checks can also bias the interviewer in the unknown applicant's favor—especially if the person was a loser and his employer built him up to try to get rid of him!

This is not, of course, intended to be an exhaustive list of all the sources of biases and prejudices. These differ from individual to individual, just as past experiences which gave birth to these attitudes differ from individual to individual. We may be biased against persons who wear blue shoes, or in favor of persons with curly hair, or against overweight individuals. The important point to remember is that each interviewer must learn to recognize his own biases and prejudices and to make certain that he tries to minimize their effect on his actions and opinions during the interview. Otherwise, he is prone to base his evaluations on unsupported conclusions, thereby losing some prime candidates for his organization, while causing the hiring of some who are less desirable.

It should be pointed out that the interviewer may also have to cope with the biases and prejudices of the candidate. Often, an interviewer will find that the candidate is clearly antagonistic toward the interviewer, for no apparent reason other than the operation of the former's prejudices. Female interviewers have encountered some particularly difficult situations. In one instance, the female employment director of a large corporation was greeted by a male applicant with the words: "Oh, I thought you were a secretary. I really would like to talk with a professional interviewer." Applicants' prejudices are also frequently apparent in cases where the applicant is considerably more experienced or at a much higher salary level than the interviewer. Similarly, white applicants occasionally resent being interviewed by nonwhite interviewers, with the result that the applicant's behavior will reflect bigotry, hostility, or the attitude that he considers himself superior to the interviewer. In each of these cases, the prejudicial attitude on the candidate's part can create a difficult situation for the interviewer. All too often the interviewer counters by calling into play biases and prejudices of his or her own against the candidate, and the interview is destined to fail. Mature interviewers understand what kind of negative effect such biases and prejudices on the part of the candidate may have on them and then discipline themselves to be objective so that the climate of the interview and the subsequent evaluation of the candidate will not be contaminated.

The Perceptual Field

Interviewers often jump to conclusions without supportive facts because they perceive other individuals incorrectly. There are many perceptual phenomena that cause us to see people and situations differently from the way they may really be or from the way others perceive them. These phenomena result from a composite of all our experiences and attitudes and are a form of bias so subtle that the untrained person is rarely able to detect their presence. Some of the most common perceptual phenomena that lead interviewers to evaluate applicants inaccurately are listed below.

Grouping. The tendency to group persons or things that appear to be similar.

Closure. The perceptual phenomenon akin to trying to close a gap in a circle to make it complete. Thus, if we see many things we dislike in a person, we tend to assume we will dislike everything about that person.

The "Halo Effect." The tendency to assume almost everything about a person is good because we like that person. This is a special kind of closure.

Internal Factors. A person's values, interests, beliefs, and motivations that tend to distort one's perceptions. Things that are important to us, and those that we value, are the ones we perceive most clearly. These same values are the ones we use to evaluate others.

Set. The expectancy to see a certain thing. Our previous experiences prepare us to see something such as we have seen before in a similar situation. In addition to our past experience, other factors such as what we need to see or what we hope to see cause perceptual set.

Projection. The tendency to assume our own needs, feelings, and attitudes are shared by others. Projection can cause us to misinterpret the actions and motives of others rather markedly. (For example, if a person tends to exaggerate habitually, he or she perceives others as exaggerating, even though they may in fact be given to understatement.)

Stereotyping. The establishment of several ready-made, oversimplified categories of persons or objects possessing a few distinct characteristics and subsequent classification of all people or objects into one of these categories. Classification is made on the basis of a very few characteristics, and the person or object so classified is then assumed to have all the other characteristics attributed to that category.

Since these perceptual phenomena, for a given individual, are the product of his past experiences and attitudes, they are like biases and prejudices in that it is impossible to eradicate them completely or to determine to operate without them. But a wise interviewer will be aware of his own tendencies to perceive situations or persons inaccurately and will take these tendencies into account in evaluating the candidate. He will ask himself whether he actually detected certain attributes in a given candidate, or whether he merely thought he perceived these attributes because of his own unique way of looking at people, without first gathering all the facts.

The Psychological Field

The interviewer also brings with him to each interview what we might call his present "psychological field." This field consists of all the various forces within the individual which are exerting pressures in various directions at the present time. These forces may interact or conflict with each other. This pattern of forces, taken as a whole, determines the behavior of the individual at a particular moment in time. The individual will not act on the basis of the actual situation, but upon the situation as he experiences or perceives it or as it relates to other situations which are uppermost in his mind. An individual's psychological field is never constant but fluctuates much more rapidly than his biases and prejudices or even his perceptual field, since it depends upon the ever-changing forces acting upon the individual and the feelings he may have at a given moment.

For instance, one very professional interviewer claims that the hardest situation for him to handle is to interview a candidate right after he has had an unpleasant discussion with his boss and is emotionally on edge. Invariably, he says, he must watch himself, or the candidate will be in for a bad time. This interviewer is not biased against the candidate himself in these situations; he is merely reacting to the psychological forces within him, which are, for the moment, conflicting and antagonistic in general. But this interviewer has learned, through experience and introspection, to counteract this tendency. If he can delay the interview until he can calm down, he does so; if not, he tries to sharpen his awareness of his own psychological state so that he can lessen its influence on his treatment and evaluation of the candidate.

INTERVIEWER IMMATURITY— SOME SITUATIONS IT CAN CREATE

The immature interviewer is one who lets his own feelings, emotions, and desires determine the course of the interview, at the expense of both objectivity and a desirable interview climate. He has not learned to control and discipline himself in order to bring about the most effective interview possible. In the next few pages, we will describe some of the types of situations interviewer immaturity can create.

The Adversary Relationship

Karen Michaels was the top candidate in her field from a leading university. She was mature, had excellent grades, looked attractive, and answered questions without a flaw. As the interview progressed, she seemed to become much more self-assured, exuding confidence and even "cockiness." About halfway through the interview, the interviewer began asking very personal and somewhat demeaning questions. He was very persistent when Karen either avoided these questions or became flustered in attempting to answer them. Finally, the interviewer terminated the session very abruptly by saying, "Well, I'm afraid if you can't handle these simple questions, and if you refuse to answer them, you don't meet the qualifications for this position."

This interviewer had lost a very good candidate—one his company was extremely interested in hiring. Why? "This girl was just too perfect and self-assured," he commented later. "She irritated me. I wanted to show her who was boss here and who controlled the job. And I wanted to prove to her that she really wasn't as good as she thought she was."

When the tone of the interview turns into a battle between the interviewer and the candidate, there is never a winner.

The "Ego-Tripper"

The ego-tripper may appear similar to the interviewer who forms an adversary relationship, but there is a subtle difference. The ego-tripper's primary goal is to impress the applicant with his own worth, rather than to put the applicant down. The ego-tripper monopolizes the interview with tales of his own achievements and accomplishments, all of which are designed to prove that he is superior to the applicant or to other individuals in general. Often, but not always, we find the ego-tripper in a male who is interviewing a confident, intelligent female. Generally an interviewer becomes an ego-tripper when he or she feels insecure or inferior to the candidate and sets out to prove otherwise.

The "Master of Stress"

The "master of stress" deliberately tries to put the applicant under pressure by questioning his statements or disagreeing with him frequently. These barbs are intentionally placed until some kind of anger is apparent in the applicant. In many cases, he becomes so angry that he breaks off the interview. Although this may be a legitimate technique in the hands of a professional highly trained in its use, it is definitely not recommended as a technique for the untrained. The nonprofessional usually can't put out the fire he or she has started, and runs a strong risk of losing a qualified candidate through alienating him. Most dangerous of all is the interviewer who has no legitimate reason to want to induce stress (e.g., the uncovering of certain specified traits); he simply wants to appear powerful through doing so, and he enjoys watching the applicant squirm while he holds the reins. This use of the stress technique is, to say the least, dangerous and immature.

The "Sell-Yourself" Interviewer

Claire is a marketing manager who occasionally interviews sales and marketing personnel. Her approach is to sit back and say little or nothing, letting the applicant respond at will to a very general question such as "Tell me about yourself" or "Tell me why you're qualified for this job." The end result is that Claire seldom gets any information about the candidate, other than just what the candidate wishes to impart, and the most garrulous applicant gets the job.

When asked why she favors this approach, Claire commented, "I don't consider it my job to have to pry information out of these applicants. If they want the job, they have to convince me that they are right for it. If they can't sell themselves to me or if they won't make the effort to sell themselves to me, then they probably won't be any good at selling or marketing anything else either, or they don't want the job badly enough."

What Claire is overlooking, of course, is that the best qualified candidate is not necessarily the one who brags the most. Many applicants could sell a product very well, but have been taught that one does not "gush" about oneself, especially in an interview. Furthermore, most candidates don't even know what kinds of information about themselves would be of value to the interviewer; so they are unable to supply it even if they wish to. Claire needs to mature enough to see that her "job" as an interviewer includes providing the guidance the applicant needs in order to "sell" his or her qualifications.

Of course, in some cases a highly trained professional who is seeking highly aggressive sales personnel may use this "sell yourself" approach during part of the interview—especially if he is trying to fill a sales position in a highly saturated market in an urban area. His use of this approach is justified, in contrast to Claire's, because he knows just what he is trying to determine about the candidate and what he is looking for in the candidate's reactions.

There are, of course, many other situations in which the interviewer's immaturity and lack of self-understanding or self-discipline cause him to lose control of the interview. The interviewer who wishes to gain maturity will avoid these situations by analyzing his own motives and attitudes, identifying those situations in which he is less than effective, and working to overcome his deficiencies and peculiarities so that he can interview effectively and objectively.

IMPROVING INTERVIEWER EFFECTIVENESS

As we have implied repeatedly throughout this chapter, even a highly trained and experienced interviewer must continue to analyze his performance and to strive for improvement. Otherwise, he is in danger of falling into bad habits and becoming less effective than he is capable of being.

Self-Evaluation

Even experienced personnel managers may be appalled, when they evaluate their own behavior in a tape-recorded interview, to recognize the common errors they are committing. The first shock occurs when the interviewer hears his voice replayed on tape. Invariably the reaction is, "That isn't me!" Next, he usually observes his frequent use of expressions that rapidly become annoying and redundant, such as "Well, that's fine," "Very good," "I see," and so forth. If the interview has been videotaped, so that he can see as well as hear himself, he may also notice that he is indulging in nervous or distracting mannerisms, such as drumming on the desk with his fingertips or playing with a pencil throughout the interview. Often he will also notice mannerisms or reactions on the part of the candidate which he failed to pick up during the actual interview—actions, for instance, which should have given the interviewer a clue that he was making the candidate angry or uncomfortable. And the most skilled interviewers often find, to their surprise, that they make common errors such as the use of leading questions or abrupt questions.

Whether an interviewer is a professional who interviews daily or a manager who may interview once a month or less she should make it a practice to tape her interview sessions occasionally and then evaluate her own performance critically and objectively—perhaps comparing it with previous tapes to note areas of improvement or degeneration. The first step in correcting bad interviewing habits is to recognize them, and the interviewer who listens to herself occasionally has the best chance of recognizing her shortcomings before they become too ingrained to alter. If a videotape is not available, the novice interviewer might consider having a more experienced inter-

Figure 3.1   Basic Self-Evaluation Form for Interviewers

	Interviewer			
	Excellent	Good	Fair	Poor
Introduction				
Structure				
Planning				
Influence Phase				
Close				
Communication Level Throughout Interview				
Questioning				
Identification of Flags				
Meeting of Objectives				
Listening Effectiveness				
Overall Evaluation				

COMMENTS:

viewer observe some of her interviewing sessions and offer a critique of her performance.

In some states, such as California, which have right-to-privacy laws, it could cause problems if interviews are taped without the applicants' permission. Frequent taping of role-playing with a colleague could be an acceptable substitute.

Figures 3.1 and 3.2 depict forms used by instructors in the field of interviewing to evaluate the performance of their students after

Figure 3.2   Advanced Self-Evaluation Form for Interviewers

Interviewer

	Excellent	Good	Fair	Poor
Introduction				
Climate				
Planning and Organizing Ability				
Aggressiveness				
Energy Level				
Maturity				
Identification of Flags				
Meeting of Objectives				
Listening Effectiveness				
Overall Evaluation				

COMMENTS:

Did the interviewer develop the above areas in the interview?

observation. Similar forms can be used by the interviewer to evaluate his or her own performance.

The form shown in Figure 3.1 is the one used to evaluate beginning interviewing students in basic courses; Figure 3.2 is the form for more advanced students in evaluation courses. Some terms used in these forms may be unfamiliar to the reader, but they will be clarified in forthcoming chapters.

In addition to rating herself on the categories listed on the evaluation sheets, the interviewer should criticize her own interviews with the following points in mind:

> Did I follow my preinterview plan?
>
> Did the interview ever degenerate into mere irrelevant conversation?
>
> Were my preinterview objectives accomplished? If not, why not?
>
> Was I adequately prepared for this interview?
>
> Was the applicant satisfied with the interview, or did he or she leave confused, disgruntled, or upset?
>
> Did I manage to make the applicant feel comfortable enough to communicate freely?
>
> Is my questioning technique awkward and stilted, or is it smooth, with a logical transition from one series of questions to another?
>
> Am I falling into any bad habits, such as failing to listen, missing flags, repeating annoying phrases, repeating questions which have already been answered?

An interviewer who is critical of her own performance may never be completely satisfied, but she will notice gradual improvement in her interviewing techniques over a period of time if she is completely objective in her periodic self-evaluations and if she strives for improvement in those areas where she fell short of her goals.

Training

More and more companies and organizations, including various governmental agencies, are realizing that their managers and personnel people need professional help in building and maintaining their interviewing skills. The novice interviewer can progress only so far by learning from his own mistakes, and all too often it is impossible for him to learn through the example of a highly trained interviewer within his organization. Like any other skill or art, the art of interviewing is best mastered through the direct and intensive tutelage of a professional interviewing instructor.

In recent years, fortunately, such instruction has become available, both in the form of seminars at leading universities and through in-house classes sponsored by companies and organizations just for their own employees. In the latter, the company or organization brings in an interviewing pro for a week or so to teach interviewing to all employees who interview, but especially to managers who do interviewing as only a part of their overall responsibilities. Only through such intensive instruction combined with the instructor's personal observation of each interviewer in action followed by individual critiques and instruction can an interviewer really master the finer points and techniques of the art in a relatively brief period of time.

Courses and seminars for interviewers are now available for both novice and advanced interviewers and can be further tailored to suit the organization's needs, taking into account the structure of the organization, the types of employees they seek, and so forth. In addition, of course, the instruction can be tailored to fit the specific needs of each individual enrolled in the class.

Such instruction is not inexpensive if it is performed by a reliable and competent professional in the field, but it pays for itself many times over by eliminating costly errors in hiring. A corporation could easily save several times the cost of such a course if it enables them to hire just one outstanding employee that a less competent interviewer might have overlooked or if it prevents them from taking on just one "loser" who is unqualified for the job.

Companies or organizations of any size, then, are urged to give their interviewers the benefit of instruction from an interviewing professional, either by sending them to a public seminar or by hiring the professional to come right into the company to study its interviewing needs and then prepare a tailormade course for its employees who interview.

Keeping Score

An effective interviewer won't stop with selection and placement on the job. He will keep track of employees he has recommended for hiring, in order to assess the accuracy of his recommendations. He will want to know:

How are these employees doing after a period of time with the company? The interviewer, through observation or through

talking with the employee's supervisor, will want to find out
how the employee has performed so far, how he gets along
with his co-workers, how he likes his job, and what are his
possibilities for advancement. Do his job attitudes and performance bear out the interviewer's original evaluation, or was
he mistaken in several important areas? Should he have rejected the candidate or recommended him for a higher-level
position?

Have some of the employees he recommended left the company,
either because their work was unsatisfactory or because they
disliked the job? The interviewer will discuss with supervisors
the reasons for certain of his "hires" leaving the organization,
closely scrutinizing his screening and interviewing procedures
to see where he might have been misled in his original evaluation. He will keep a file on his turnovers and periodically
review his "batting average" with supervision and management. At the end of the year, he will reassess his score, evaluating his overall performance in relation to the turnover
record of the total organization.

The successful interviewer is one who can use his skills, techniques, and understanding of applicants to maintain or improve his
organization's high employment standards. The future and success
of every organization depends not only on the skills of the company's
professional interviewers, but also on every manager's skills in handling the occasional interview. Even if you are responsible for only
one hiring recommendation or decision a year, that one decision
could have great impact on your company's future—so take a hard
look at your own performance, get some training, sharpen your
interviewing skills, and make that one decision count!

Chapter 4
Preparation
for the Interview

Interviewing experts find it a constant source of amazement that many managers and high-level executives who are extremely meticulous in their planning and execution of business operations tend to approach something as complex as an interview with an exceedingly casual and nonchalant attitude. With almost no planning or preparation time and with very little warm-up, they sit down with a candidate, scan his or her application, and toss out a few questions off the tops of their heads. At the end of fifteen minutes or half an hour, they flip a coin or use a "gut feeling" to assess the applicant. Needless to say, this does not prove to be an effective way of selecting employees. Even worse, it can easily turn off the candidates you really want to hire. For an example, let's look in on an executive who is "too busy" to spruce up on his interviewing or to give it any forethought.

John MacNeil, vice-president of Swift Electronics, had experienced a nerve-wracking week. He was in the final phase of a value analysis presentation for the Air Materiel Command of his new airborne computer. He had returned from Washington the night before and had arrived in his office late that morning. He had just finished briefing the company president on where they stood in the contract competition. He hadn't seen the application of Jim Johnson before picking it up from his secretary on his way into the office that morning. Even then, he had only skimmed over the information on the first few lines. He had also been too preoccupied with important decisions to spend any time studying the file prepared by the personnel department, although it had been on his desk well before his trip to Washington. He did know that this young engineer had an excellent reputation within his field and that many people within the company were impressed with him and eager to have him join the company. The hiring stamp of approval or rejection rested on John's shoulders.

It was this situation that provided the backdrop for the interview young Jim encountered. Fifteen minutes after he entered MacNeil's office, Jim left in a huff, grabbed his coat, and failed to say anything to the receptionist as he headed for the visitors' parking lot.

Jim was a candidate for a supervisory position in the Airborne Computer Division of Swift. He had been working for a competitor and had been recruited through an agency for this opening. He had liked everything he had seen so far at Swift—the people, the benefits, the working conditions, the salary; all were attractive. But the vice-president's demeanor, his approach, and his obvious lack of interest gave Jim an entirely new outlook on the company and the job.

MacNeil's initial remarks to Jim were unthinking. He was obviously preoccupied with the world of defense contracts and gave the impression that the valuable time he was wasting on Jim could have been more profitably spent in tending to business. He obviously didn't listen to the answers Jim gave to his questions. Much of the time, he didn't even look at Jim, but at the application blank on his desk. His questions concerning Jim's background were interpreted as being very personal and insulting and often irrelevant to the available position. Furthermore, his questions indicated to Jim that MacNeil had not been interested enough to read his application prior to the interview or to review the information that had already been provided in great detail to personnel. And twice, Jim's train of thought had been interrupted in midsentence—once when MacNeil answered his phone and chatted briefly with an employee and once when MacNeil's secretary opened the door to say that a co-worker was waiting to see him. When Jim asked a couple of questions about the position and its benefits, MacNeil's vague reply convinced him that, although the position was in MacNeil's division, he really knew very little about it.

Jim Johnson was a reasonable young man, but the events of this interview really bothered him. He decided to accept an offer from

Acme Electronics, even though, up to the interview with MacNeil, it had been a second choice.

Meanwhile, shortly after Jim had left the office, MacNeil received a call from Al Monk, the department head who had previously interviewed Jim and who was anxious to hire him.

"What did you think, Mac?" Al asked eagerly. "Is Jim the man for the job?"

"Well," replied MacNeil, scratching his head reflectively, "he seemed like a nice kid. Maybe a little moody. Seems like I couldn't get him to open up and talk to me man to man . . . you know, give me the low-down on himself. And he seemed sort of put out when he left. Maybe he's having second thoughts."

"Hmm . . . that's funny. When I talked to him, he seemed very frank and willing to talk openly. What kinds of information were you trying to zero in on, Mac?"

"Oh, you know. The normal things. Background, and so on." MacNeil sounded a little less sure of himself now.

"Well, specifically what were you trying to find out that we hadn't already established from my interview or from his previous background information?" Al persisted.

MacNeil was stymied. If pressed, he would have to admit that he had no idea what he was trying to find out beyond the information already available; he had no idea, in fact, what information was available and what was not.

The result would have been the same if Al had asked him any one of a number of questions: "How do you think he shapes up against the qualifications we have in mind for this position?" "How does his past track record compare with our needs and job objectives?" "Do you think his long-range goals fit in with the career pattern we plan on?" "How do you think he'll get along with the other guys in the department?" "In your opinion, can he supervise?" "Is he sold on the job?" Chances are the answer to all these questions, if MacNeil is an honest man, would have been "I have no idea." And the reason MacNeil would have no idea is that he didn't do his homework before the interview, either by studying the candidate's background and the position or by preparing himself mentally to devote his attention to the applicant and to establish a rapport with him. Because he had no objectives, no interview plan, and little prior information, he had accomplished nothing at all in the interview except to lose the candidate for reasons he would never understand. Even if he had not lost the candidate, he would have gathered little or no information that would have enabled him to make an astute decision to hire or not to hire. About the most he could have added to the information already obtained by others was his erroneous judgment that the applicant was moody—and small wonder, in the face of his treatment by MacNeil!

These occurrences are repeated hundreds of times daily with endless variation simply because interviewers fail to keep elementary interviewing skills in their repertoires or to plan, prior to the actual interview, how those skills can best be utilized in a particular situation.

Let's take a look, now, at the other side of the coin—an interviewing pro who knows that adequate preparation is the only solid basis upon which to build an interview. Sharon Dixon is an assistant employment manager for a medium-sized Eastern manufacturer. Although she is a full-time interviewing professional, the steps she follows in setting herself up for an important interview with a potential sales manager can serve as preparation guidelines for anyone who interviews, even on a very occasional basis.

STUDYING PREINTERVIEW INFORMATION

Sharon knows that she must do her homework before she meets the applicant. She needs to know as much as possible about the job, the company as a whole, and the individual applicant who is applying for that job. Only with this information in mind can she plan an interview that will give her the maximum opportunity of making the best possible match between the applicant and the position.

Work Conditions and Job Specifications

Unless Sharon has a fairly intimate knowledge of the job requirements, the conditions, and environment in which the employee will be expected to work and the overall atmosphere of the company, she will find it impossible to assess the ability of the candidate to fit into the job. She will, in addition, find it difficult to sell the candidate on the job if she does determine he or she is right for it. Much of this information on job needs is developed by Sharon in a meeting with the department manager or supervisor who will be making the hiring decision. This step is essential for two reasons: It not only provides Sharon with the data she needs, but also helps the manager by forcing him to think about the characteristics that should be possessed by the candidate he hires.

In this meeting, Sharon tries to get answers to many questions.

What exact duties must the candidate be able to perform? What specific skills will this require? What other experiences or abilities would be desirable but not essential? Will the job include any unusual aspects, such as extensive travel or frequent overtime? What is the "mood" of the department: relaxed or formal, highly-structured or laissez-faire? What types of people will the employee have to get along with on a peer level? In a subordinate or supervisory capacity?

Sharon will also want to note any problems peculiar to this position in the past. (Have the last three employees in this job lasted less than a year each? Did the last employee resign in a huff? Are there employee problems among the subordinates to this position? If so, Sharon should try to determine the cause of these irregularities.)

Sharon also reviews the salary range and fringe benefits for the position as well as for the entire labor market in which she is competing. She needs to know not only the opening salary and benefits her candidate can expect in the position and his or her potential for increases in the years ahead, but also how these stack up against what other companies are offering for similar services. If her company's salaries tend to be somewhat low, for example, she may need to place more emphasis on other benefits or on nonmonetary compensations. If the salary for this particular position is generous compared with other salaries in the field, she will want to emphasize the excellent financial opportunity her firm offers.

Sharon, as a professional interviewer, will probably already have a well-grounded understanding of the company—its structure, the organizational pressures on employees, the heirarchy or echelons of command, the political groups within the various areas of the organization, and the services or products the organization delivers. She should also, of course, have intimate knowledge of the various jobs available in the organization or those that might be available in the future—especially at the skilled and professional levels. Surprisingly, the need for this type of knowledge is frequently overlooked. But many times, an astute interviewer who has such knowledge will discover that while the applicant may be unqualified or unsuited for the position for which he is being interviewed, he may be an outstanding candidate for another job within the company. Without this knowledge and flexibility, a promising potential employee would be lost.

Of course, since Sharon is a professional interviewer, she makes it an important part of her job to keep abreast of much of this information. She doesn't have to start from scratch every time she is scheduled to interview an applicant. A busy executive who conducts an occasional interview may be unable to keep up with all this information on a day-to-day basis, but she can arrange frequent briefings to keep her filled in on these types of information.

Once Sharon has gathered all the facts pertaining to the particular position she is trying to fill, she prepares a job specification sheet. This might be structured much like the one in Figure 4.1, so that all Sharon needs to do is to fill in the blanks with the pertinent information. Under the "Miscellaneous" heading, she is careful to note any unusual aspects of the position or problems associated with it which have not been covered under the other headings. When she has finished preparing the specification sheet, she should have a reasonably accurate and concise outline of the type of position and work atmosphere the candidate is expected to fit into and some of the personal characteristics he or she should possess. We'll discuss these further in the following pages.

It should be emphasized that the type of job specification sheet we are talking about here is solely for the use of the interviewer and any other representatives of the organization who will be involved in the hiring decision. This type of job specification sheet should not be confused with the type that some organizations prepare for wage and salary considerations. In the latter type, very specific and factual skills and abilities are indicated, together with the person's actual activities on the job. In the kind we are advocating here, on the other hand, we are more concerned with determining the general *type* of employee we need.

No doubt many managers who interview occasionally will find that position descriptions or job specification sheets have already been prepared for them elsewhere in the organization. Even if this is the case, the person who is to do the actual interviewing will want to verify the accuracy of the information on the sheet and to add a few notes of his or her own, based on personal observation of the environment and atmosphere into which the candidate is to be placed.

The average manager may complain that he or she is too busy to handle all the interview preparation advocated in this approach. In the long run, however, if you add up the time spent in handling the problems of the quickly selected "misfit," not to mention the time and money spent in additional recruiting for the misfit's replacement, you will find that a little preparatory work saves hundreds of valuable hours.

In conjunction with the job specification sheet, Sharon reviews a list of desirable characteristics for employees in the particular broad "job family" which this position represents. Figure 4.2 shows an encapsulated list of this type for the "Sales" family of jobs.

Figure 4.1   The Job Specification Sheet

POSITION TITLE:

TECHNICAL REQUIREMENTS:
Education:*
1. Essential
2. Desirable

Experience:
1. Essential minimums (Be realistic and evaluate carefully.)
2. Optional background—desirable but not essential

POSITION STRUCTURE:
1. What is the person expected to produce?
2. On what schedule are they expected to produce it?
3. Is this position closely supervised?
4. Will there be contact with those in other departments and/or with customers or clients? How much?
5. What is the organizational environment (high pressure, fast paced, understaffed)?
6. What are the decision- and/or policy-making requirements?

PERSONAL REQUIREMENTS:
1. What are some personal attributes or characteristics the successful candidate should have to fill the current job? (E.g., high energy level, high level of verbal skills, maturity, leadership skills, etc.)
2. What type of professional versatility or growth potential should the candidate possess?

COMPENSATION FACTORS:
1. Salary
2. Fringe benefits

MISCELLANEOUS:

*Note: most organizations tend to overstate educational requirements, particularly for entry-level positions.

In the introductory chapter, we alluded to the need for individual organizations to establish their own criteria for various jobs and job families within the company, in order to make their interviewing process valid. An excellent place to begin within a single organization is to reach a consensus on lists of desirable abilities and characteristics for each broad category of job, such as the one we have just looked

Figure 4.2 Desirable Characteristics for Sales Employees

EFFECT ON CUSTOMERS

1. *Appearance:* Does the individual exhibit neatness in dress and grooming as it relates to the *impact* of the person on the observer? (Caution: Minimize personal feelings and consider the results of possible counseling.)
2. *Personality:* Does the individual give the impression of being confident but not cocky or know-it-all?
3. *Communication skills:* Does the individual have: (a) the ability to listen and (b) the ability to express himself or herself clearly and concisely?
4. *Awareness:* Is the individual sensitive and perceptive to the situation, the environment, and the other individual?
5. *Interpersonal relations:* Is the individual flexible enough to relate with different levels or types of customers? Can he or she adjust to periods of no personal contact?

JOB-RELATED ATTITUDES

1. *Planning and organizing ability:* Will the individual organize his or her time efficiently when unsupervised?
2. *Aggressiveness:* Is this a competitive individual who is willing to close the sale?
3. *Drive:* Does he or she have the self-motivation to meet schedules without close supervision?
4. *Work ethic:* How well does the individual face up to his or her responsibilities?
5. *Realistic motivation:* Are both the long-term and short-term goals of the individual compatible with his or her abilities?
6. *Goal vs. task orientation:* Would the individual view "calling on a physician" as a task or a goal?
7. *Energy level:* Does the individual have the physical and mental stamina to stand up under a tough sales job?
8. *Maturity:* Can the individual learn from failure, or does he or she blame others?
9. *Tolerance to failure:* Is every "turn-down" by a customer a blow to the individual's ego and will it destroy the individual psychologically?

at, and to see that all interviewers refer to these lists when recruiting these kinds of employees. The list of traits provided here is offered as a model, with the understanding that each organization may find that its emphases, for the same job family, may vary somewhat from the model. These variations in desirable traits may occur from company to company for any number of reasons: differences in organizational structure, the type of person managing the facility and his or her style of management, the varying ways in which duties are apportioned, or fluctuations between companies or even among divisions within the same company in the amount or types of pressure inherent in the work atmosphere. And, of course, the model given here deals with only one of a wide range of job families. It must be left to each organization to define the job families it utilizes and then to delineate, through careful research and soul-searching, those traits that have proven necessary for success within each family *in this particular organization.* Great care should be exercised to avoid listing commonly accepted stereotypical traits for a job family (e.g., extreme aggressiveness for sales) if these traits have not proven to be necessary or even particularly desirable within the framework of the organization under consideration.

There are two major keys to the effectiveness of these lists of desirable traits for job families within the organization. First, these lists must be established through input from as many sources as are available. In establishing a list of traits for the sales family, for example, it would be desirable to incorporate the opinions of, say, the vice-president of sales, the sales managers, some of the salespersons themselves, and the personnel department. If records exist of former salespersons who have resigned or have been fired, their reasons for termination should also be examined for clues. While these clues cannot lead to hard and fast conclusions, they can serve as useful guidelines and as reminders to consider various characteristics that could otherwise have been overlooked.

The second key to effectiveness is the uniform application of the lists once they have been agreed upon. All persons who screen or hire applicants for a particular category of position must understand the list of abilities and characteristics and must use it in evaluating every candidate if it is to increase the validity of the organization's selection program.

Of course, even within a specific job family within a certain organization some jobs will place more emphasis on one desirable characteristic than will other jobs. In a company which makes a wide variety of electronic equipment, for instance, the most important characteristics for the salesperson who markets pocket calculators to department stores in the Chicago area may be very different from the most important characteristics for the salesperson who will market computers around the world. So once the desirable traits for the job family have been determined, there may have to be a further determination of those which should be emphasized within various branches of the job family. In a large company, this could be done formally, but more often it is left for the interviewer to determine on the basis of the job specifications and the other information he or she is able to gather about the specific position to be filled.

In Chapter 7, we will go into greater detail about the application of these lists of traits during the interviewing process.

Applicant Background

The reader probably will have noticed by now that Sharon, our model interviewer, has so far prepared for the interview solely by looking at the job. She has not yet so much as glanced at any information pertaining to the individual applicant or his background. This order is not accidental. Although many interviewers tend to start backwards, by looking at the candidate first, the most effective procedure is to know the needs of the job first (assuming, of course, that you are screening or hiring for a specific position rather than just looking for good candidates in general). Then, and only then, can the candidate be assessed in light of those needs. It is meaningless to attempt evaluation of any candidate prior to determining the standards he must meet, in terms of personality traits, background, and so forth. Unless he can be compared to such a set of optimum and specific standards, there is no way of determining whether he is "excellent," "good," "mediocre," or "bad." Even if the interviewer intends to compare the applicant's background information with the job specifications later, there is a danger in looking over the application blank or resumé first: The interviewer's own biases or his lack of knowledge about the job specifications may lead him to form a premature and erroneous judgment about the applicant's suitability for the job, and this preliminary judgment can easily color the interviewer's thinking even after a subsequent matching of background data against job specifications reveals that the early judgment was an invalid one.

Once the job specifications have been prepared and the desirable characteristics for the job family in general reviewed, Sharon is ready to look over whatever information is available to her about the applicant or applicants she will be interviewing. She can now undertake this step of her interview preparation with the assurance that it will be productive, since she can compare the *available* information about each applicant with the information *needed* in order to reach an intelligent decision about his or her suitability for the particular job available.

At this stage, the amount of information available to Sharon on a given applicant may vary considerably, depending on the situation. Any or all of the following may be available to her: the application blank or resumé of the applicant; information secured from background investigations, previous employer checks, school records, letters of recommendation, or other indicators of past performance; remarks from previous screening interviews, if any; and briefings from the company psychologist or other interviewers concerning areas of general sensitivity (although some professionals prefer not to have this latter type of information until after the in-depth interview has been conducted on the grounds that such information might tend to bias their decision).

Any of these sorts of information will help Sharon become as familiar as possible with the applicant before she ever meets him face to face. This preinterview acquaintance with the candidate will help her in two important ways: She will be better equipped to make the candidate feel at ease during the actual interview, because she will appear interested in him and will be able to converse normally without constant referral to his application blank, and she will be able to determine, before he ever arrives, what kinds of information she needs to elicit from him in order to fill the voids in her knowledge about his suitability for the position. If she fails to study and digest the available information prior to the interview, she could easily waste most of her valuable interview time in obtaining information that has already been submitted in written form or obtained through previous screening interviews, much as the "application reader" we criticized in the first chapter.

Naturally, in a preliminary screening interview on campus, none of this information may be available in advance. Although a resumé or data sheet is usually required of campus candidates, the procedure on some campuses is to have the applicant bring the data sheet with him when he arrives for the interview. If the interviewer cannot convince the placement director at the college or university that data sheets should be submitted prior to the actual interview, he or she will simply have to make the best of the situation by taking a few minutes at the start of the interview to go over the data with the student. This procedure, which we call "verification," will be discussed more fully in Chapter 10. The interviewer who must resort to reviewing the applicant's background while he or she is present will find it doubly valuable to have the position requirements firmly in mind, so that an instantaneous mental comparison may be made between the available data and the job requirements, and a rapid decision can be reached regarding the types of information still needed to reach a decision.

ESTABLISHING INTERVIEW OBJECTIVES

Once Sharon has a clear idea of the job qualifications and has reviewed the available information on the interviewee, she is ready to do some planning as to how the interview itself should be conducted. As a professional, she takes this aspect of her job most seriously. She realizes that an interview without a plan can easily turn into a hit-or-miss proposition, with very little accomplished during the allotted time.

This is where Sharon establishes her objectives for the interview. As we discussed in the opening chapter, viable and clearly delineated objectives are essential if the interview is to accomplish its overall purpose of matching the candidate to the job.

Of course, in every interview, Sharon will want to meet certain minimal objectives. The first might be to make the applicant feel comfortable and to establish a rapport with him, so that he will act naturally and supply information candidly. Another objective will be to answer the candidate's questions about the job and the organization, so that he leaves the interview feeling that his own needs for information have been met. And a third objective might be to sell the candidate on the job or on the company, in the event that the candidate meets hiring criteria. These objectives are very broad and general in that they apply to almost any conceivable interview situation; the objectives themselves do not vary from candidate to candidate, although the specific means employed in reaching these objectives may well vary with each individual.

On the other hand, Sharon's objectives for the body or information-gathering portion of the interview will be tailored to the specific applicant and the specific position. They will reflect what Sharon feels she needs to know in order to recommend the hiring or rejection of this candidate, and they will be based specifically on her comparison of the available applicant information with her job specification sheet and her desirable characteristics list for the job family in question.

Like the general in Chapter 1 who wanted to conquer the world, Sharon must establish broad informational objectives and then subdivide these into more specific and discrete objectives until she reaches the point where her objectives are well defined and manageable within the framework of the interview. For a particular interview, Sharon's broad objectives could read like this:

1. Substantiate certain information on the application and determine the reasons and methods behind certain activities.
2. Obtain new information to fill existing voids in the applicant's background.
3. Try to get an accurate picture of the "whole" individual.

More specifically, Sharon might decide her objectives are to:

1. Substantiate the applicant's report that he graduated at the top of his class in marketing at the University of Kansas, that he was responsible for an entire sales division at Ace Corporation, and that he is now taking graduate courses in market research, with an emphasis on determining why and how these things were done.
2. Obtain new information to determine what the applicant's exact responsibilities were in his job at Ace Corporation, how involved he is in the numerous outside activities he listed on his resumé, what he did during his two years in the Army, what he did during a three-year period that is not accounted for on his application, and whether he hopes to change his career path once he has attained a graduate degree in marketing.
3. Get a feeling for the applicant's career goals, his attitudes about managing people, his energy level, his ability to take constructive criticism, his ability to work without a great deal of direction, his overall compatibility with the extremely gregarious people who would be in his department, and his ability and willingness to work long and irregular hours, often away from home.

By spelling out her objectives in this manner, Sharon has simultaneously identified the kinds of information she must obtain in order to meet them. She must now review them to determine whether they appear to be viable. Is it reasonable to expect to accomplish each objective, considered separately? If so, is it reasonable to expect to accomplish *all* of them in the amount of time allotted for the interview? If the answer to this latter question is negative, then Sharon will have to decide which of the objectives are most important to her, and those that are less crucial to the decision will have to be given a lower priority, to be pursued only if time permits after those of higher priority have been fulfilled.

Inexperienced interviewers, if they establish objectives at all, often establish an overwhelming number of them and then feel frustrated when it turns out to be impossible to meet even a fraction of their goals within a brief interview. However, it is much better to have too many objectives and run out of time, than to have so few that the last half of the interview dies for lack of purpose. The key here is to decide which of your many objectives should receive top priority, to keep lower-priority objectives in reserve in case you fulfill the more important ones before the time runs out, and to remember that if you end up with some of your objectives unmet, you are probably still many steps ahead of the interviewer who never had any objectives in the first place. There is probably not an interviewer alive who has met all of his objectives all of the time, but at least when the interview is over he knows what information he needed that he was unable, for one reason or another, to obtain. Sometimes, there is valuable information to be obtained from the simple fact that a certain objective could not be met or a certain type of data could not be extracted from the applicant.

Once Sharon has decided that her interview objectives are viable and has established priorities for them, she can plan exactly how she will attempt to meet them. How, in other words, will she go after the information she wants? As we will see later on, one method she can use is the cone system. By programming her objectives into "cones," she can be sure to gather information on the broad topics that interest her most and those that allow her the greatest opportunity to probe for attitudes. Within each broad topic she chooses to explore, she can plan, before the interview ever begins, the specific points she will want to pursue in greater depth. The way in which objectives can be incorporated into the cone system of interviewing will be discussed in greater detail in Chapters 6 and 7.

PLANNING FOR EFFICIENT TIME MANAGEMENT

By now, Sharon has a fairly clear idea of her interview objectives and the subjects she needs to pursue in order to meet them. Now she must decide how to allocate her time during the interview so that she has the best chance of covering the most important topics during the allotted period.

She must remember at this point that she has some objectives other than the information-gathering type we have just discussed. She also has the objectives of making the candidate feel comfortable and establishing a rapport with him, filling his need for information about the company, selling him on the job, and so forth. The interview must be planned with these objectives as well as the informational ones in mind. The effective interview has a basic structure with several separate and distinct stages for the accomplishment of these various kinds of objectives.

The Interview Profile

Figure 4.3 shows the profile of a 30-minute interview and indicates about how much time should be allotted for each stage in an interview of this length. Let's examine each phase briefly, although we will deal with the mechanics of each later.

The introduction and the structure of the interview are aimed toward meeting noninformational objectives. The introduction is that period of time set aside at the beginning of the interview for the interviewer to get acquainted with the candidate and to put her at ease. This is where good communication is established; the introduction sets the tone for the remainder of the interview.

After approximately 5 minutes, in a 30-minute interview, the introduction is followed by the brief structure phase. This stage is simply an outline of the procedure that will be followed during the rest of the interview. It serves to put the candidate even more at ease by letting her know generally what is going to happen and about how long it will take and by assuring her that her own needs for information will be met before the session is ended.

The body of the interview is sometimes called the "assessment phase," and it is viewed as the heart of the interviewing process. It is here, in the body of the interview, that the interviewer fulfills his primary objectives by gathering the information that will help him determine whether the applicant fits the job. If he has chosen to use the cone approach to interviewing, described in Chapter 6, it is during this phase that he will bring his cones into play. When planning the use of time during the interview, the interviewer can profitably break down the total amount of time allotted for the body of the interview; he may want to subdivide this 15 minutes, for example, into three 5-

Figure 4.3 The Interview Profile

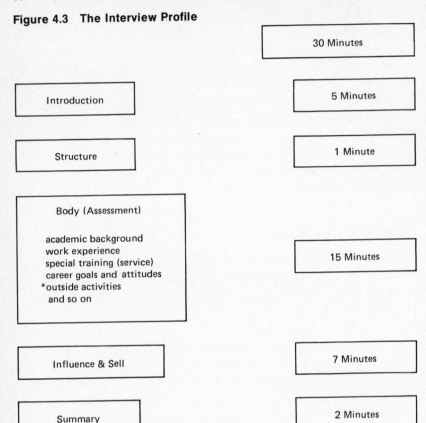

	30 Minutes
Introduction	5 Minutes
Structure	1 Minute
Body (Assessment) academic background work experience special training (service) career goals and attitudes *outside activities and so on	15 Minutes
Influence & Sell	7 Minutes
Summary	2 Minutes

*To be avoided in states such as California, where right-to-privacy laws require that inquiries be job-related.

minute cones, so that he knows just how much time he has to pursue each broad topic on his agenda.

In general, during the body of the interview, the interviewer will be seeking three kinds of information. The first is factual background information—details about the applicant's schooling, skills, previous job experience, outside activities, and so forth. This is the kind of information that could be obtained through direct questioning (although, as we shall see later, there are alternative ways of obtaining it that make for better communication). The second is information about the individual's attitudes, feelings, and traits, such as maturity, creativity, drive, and so forth. Most information of this sort is not accessible through direct questioning. (The interviewer cannot ask an applicant, for instance, "Are you mature?") Instead, these attitudes and characteristics must be ascertained through careful evaluation of the applicant's responses to other questions. The third type of information will be based on judgments that the interviewer should be able to make simply as a result of spending some time observing the candidate—her appearance, communication skills, and surface personality.

Of course, the exact nature of the information the interviewer needs to obtain during the body of the interview will have been determined earlier, when he compared job specifications and desirable traits for this particular job family with the information already available on the candidate and formulated his objectives.

The influence and sell portion of the interview follows the body. During this stage, both the applicant and the interviewer have a chance to meet some of their objectives. The applicant has her chance to become the questioner and to find out what she wants to know about the position, the organization, the product or service that she would be dealing with if she were to accept the job, and the types of people she would be working with. The interviewer, in addition to answering the applicant's queries, has the chance to sell the applicant on the company and the job. This is where the interviewer goes all out to persuade the candidate that this is the job and the organization in which she should pursue her career—providing, of course, that the candidate meets the established requirements and is likely to be offered the job.

The final stage of the interview is a brief summary, which is directed more toward meeting the candidate's needs than toward fulfilling the interviewer's objectives. The summary, as its name implies, merely summarizes what has transpired and leaves the applicant with the feeling that the interview has been brought to a logical and successful close, that a good relationship has been established between the two participants, and that she knows what to expect as the next step in the hiring process.

Naturally, the interviewer must remain somewhat flexible in his timing as he conducts these various stages of the interview. If he has allotted 5 minutes for the introductory phase, for example, he can't consult a stopwatch and cut the applicant off in midsentence when the 5-minute interval has expired. He may even want to decide, at the end of the 5 minutes, that the introductory phase should be deliberately extended in order to give the tense applicant a little more time to relax and to give himself a better chance to establish a rapport with the applicant before beginning the assessment phase of the interview. By the same token, if the interviewer has planned to spend 5 minutes during the body of the interview talking about the candidate's first job and has discovered at the end of 2 minutes on the subject that he has all the information he needs on this particular topic, it would be fruitless to use up the remaining 3 minutes allotted. He would be far better off to abandon the exhausted topic ahead of schedule and move on to the next scheduled subject, which may well prove so informative that he will want to dwell on it for more than its allotted 5 minutes. Thus the interview profile set up by the interviewer is not meant to be so rigid that it will hamper him; it is, rather, designed to serve as only an organizational tool to aid him in seeing that all stages are covered and all his objectives met before he runs out of time.

In a longer interview—say, a hiring-decision interview at the executive level—all the stages might be somewhat longer than in the 30-minute profile outlined here, but most of the extra time would probably go into the body of the interview and, to a lesser extent, into the "influence and sell" portion.

SETTING THE STAGE

Let's return for a moment to Sharon, our interviewing pro. When Sharon has completed all her homework—studying job specifications and applicant background, setting objectives, and allocating the time during the interview—prior to the candidate's arrival for his interview, she still has one task to take care of before he shows up at the door. She must set the stage so that the physical environment for the interview will be conducive to good communication. The top priority here is ensuring privacy for as long as the interview will take. Almost without exception, a candidate will become nervous and inhibited when the interviewer interrupts the interviewing process to answer phone calls or to talk with visitors, and the flow of communication soon diminishes to a trickle. Even if the candidate does manage to retain his poise and keep talking, the interviewer's concentration will be broken, decreasing the likelihood that he will grasp the significance of what the candidate is saying. Sharon always makes arrangements to have her phone calls held while she is interviewing and takes any necessary precautions against interruptions. In budgeting time, it is imperative to arrange for privacy for anywhere from 45 minutes to two hours—the anticipated length of the interview plus a little extra in case it runs longer than expected. Sharon also finds it convenient, if she can manage it, to have a few more uninterrupted minutes immediately after the applicant leaves. She uses this time to make some notes about the candidate while his comments and her impressions are still fresh in her mind.

Sharon also tries to keep other extraneous noise and confusion at a minimum during the interview, although of course this cannot always be perfectly controlled. She is fortunate to have a private office in a quiet corner of the building with a secretary who can intercept her telephone calls and visitors, but she often runs into problems when she has to interview on a college campus or in some other location. The following matters might be considered by the interviewer who is attempting to set the stage for an effective interview:

If your office is not in a quiet location or if it cannot be made private, attempt to borrow someone else's office which meets these criteria for the duration of the interview.

If you have no secretary or assistant who can turn callers away, consider a "Do Not Disturb" sign for your door.

If music is piped into your office, turn it off or to its lowest volume if possible.

If your office window looks out on a scene of bustling confusion, such as a construction site or a busy sidewalk, close the drapes or shades to keep the outside activity from competing for your attention. When it is impossible to shut off such a view, try to seat yourself and the applicant in locations that will not encourage your focusing on the scene outside.

Try to avoid scheduling interviews during times when excessive activity will be taking place just outside your office—right before or after lunch hour, for example, or on the day when new carpet is being laid in the hallway. Also avoid hours when whistles are blown, announcements made over the public address system, and so forth, if you are able to determine when these interruptions are most likely to happen. Many an interview has been ruined by a fire drill!

When an unforeseen or unavoidable interruption does occur, don't let it capture your attention. Keep your interest riveted on the candidate. If you see that the interruption has confused or upset the candidate or that her attention has wandered, apologize briefly, explain the nature of the interruption if this is necessary, and draw her firmly back into the conversation.

By the time the applicant enters Sharon's office, she has already laid much of the groundwork for a successful and effective interview through the use of prior planning and study, time management, and an environment conducive to in-depth communication. No interviewer—not even the busiest executive—can afford to slight these all-important preparatory phases of the interviewing process.

Chapter 5
Interaction with the Applicant

In a previous chapter, we discussed the need for communication in the interview that goes beyond the superficial and that is made up almost entirely of relevant information. This does not mean, however, that we can expect the opening moments of the interview to immediately consist of communication at this depth and level of relevance. These goals can only be achieved after the two participants in the interview have begun to feel comfortable with one another and to establish a rapport. This requires, on the part of the applicant, a willingness to speak freely with the interviewer and, on the part of the interviewer, a rapidly acquired understanding of the applicant as an individual which will enable him or her to bring about this willingness.

HOW THE APPLICANT COMES TO THE INTERVIEW

There are few set rules for establishing a rewarding relationship with a candidate, because each candidate arrives at the interview with his own personality characteristics, his own background and experiences, and the many other traits that make him a unique individual. It will be incumbent upon the interviewer to assess from the application data and in the beginning stages of the interview what type of individual he or she is dealing with and to tailor his or her approach accordingly.

Applicants may be old or young, experienced or applying for a first job, timid, self-confident, or egotistical to the point of trying to "put down" the interviewer. They may be on their first interview; they may have had so many interviews that they are well practiced; or they may have been coached on how to act and what answers to give in the interview. Some may be participating in this interview because they just wish to gain experience in taking interviews, rather than because they are especially interested in your job or your company. Others may be almost desperate to be hired for this particular job. A few may have had such bad experiences during other interviews that they are hostile. In Chapter 8, we will discuss in more detail some techniques for handling various types of "problem" applicants, and Chapter 10 will also touch on special problems most often encountered during campus interviewing. But for now, the interviewer should be aware that he cannot expect any success in establishing a free flow of communication until he has determined some of the unique characteristics and experiences that the applicant brings to the interview.

In addition to his set characteristics and background, each applicant brings with him to the interview his present psychological field, just as the interviewer does (see Chapter 3). This is the field of interacting and conflicting forces and pressures which determine the individual's behavior at a given point in time and causes him to experience, perceive, and interpret situations in a constantly changing manner.

The ability of the interviewer to understand, predict, or influence an applicant's behavior, then, requires that the interviewer gain insight into the various positive and negative forces that comprise the applicant's psychological field at the moment. We must develop our ability to visualize and experience the situation as he does. This is not easy, of course, and one person can never gain a perfect understanding of another's psychological field, but progress can be made toward this end through a combination of astute evaluation of the known facts about the applicant, skillful questioning, and sympathetic listening with a real effort toward understanding of the individual's attitudes.

The Goals of the Applicant

The goals of the applicant, as they pertain to the job in question, are a special aspect of his total psychological field. Although they are only a small part of his total field, they are very dominant forces during the interview, because the applicant's thoughts and behavior at this particular point in time are focused on job-related topics.

Let's take the case of Sam, who has come to interview for a job as a pharmaceutical salesman, traveling extensively over a wide territory. Let's assume that you, as the interviewer, know that Sam is married and has been a graduate student in social work but has not yet received a graduate degree. You don't yet know why Sam is quitting school. You also don't know that he is considering part-time work at night in a service station, so that he can continue schooling.

Sam's ultimate choice will be influenced by the positive and negative aspects of the situation as they appear to him. Perhaps more important to you, the interviewer, his feelings about the job he accepts and his potential for success in that job will hinge upon his own interpretation of the situation's positive and negative aspects. In other words, Sam may have the perfect experience and background for the job, but if he does not perceive it as fulfilling most of his goals, he will probably not perform in it as well as he might. Unless you are able to determine, through skillful communication on a deep level, what Sam's goals are, you will be unable to accurately evaluate Sam's potential for success on the job. You will also have difficulty in determining why Sam makes certain types of statements during the interview and in understanding the reasons for various attitudes Sam expresses.

In Sam's case, there are many goals that he would like to fulfill. Meanwhile, as he sees it, there are three alternative courses of action open to him: taking a full-time sales job, staying in school full time, or combining a menial job with graduate study. None of these alternatives will meet all his goals, according to his perception. His dilemma might be diagrammed as shown in Figure 5.1.

What the diagram does not show is that Sam undoubtedly attaches more worth or importance to some goals than to others, and this will also influence his behavior. If he feels great pressure to support his wife entirely and to let her quit work, for example, this may overshadow his needs to reach any or all of the other goals. Furthermore, the relative weight of each goal may fluctuate from time to time, depending upon other forces and pressures that are operative in Sam's life.

In order to understand Sam's behavior and attitudes, then, the interviewer needs to determine and understand Sam's goals. This not only will help him interpret Sam's statements and match him to the available job, but it will also enable him to keep communication flowing more smoothly during the interview. As we will see in Chapter

Figure 5.1   Sam's Dilemma—Goals vs. Alternatives

Positive Goals

Alternatives	Positive Goals
	Increase status at present
	Enable wife to quit work
	Increase family's total income
Sales job	Avoid feeling totally dependent on wife
Sam	Keep circle of friends at school
Service station and graduate school	Avoid the "rat race" of the business world
Graduate school only	Get graduate degree
	Prepare for career helping others
	Allow ample time to spend with wife

8, it will also aid the interviewer in selling the applicant on the company and the job, if he should decide that Sam is the candidate he wishes to hire.

ESTABLISHING A PERMISSIVE CLIMATE

The first portions of the interview, often called the introduction and structure phases, serve primarily to establish a relationship between the interviewer and the applicant and to lay the groundwork for free communication in the stages that follow. Little significant information-gathering takes place during these first two stages.

The initial phases of the interview—especially the introduction—

are critical to the whole communication process. As such, they may well be the most important portion of the interview. If the proper atmosphere is not created during these first few minutes, the candidate may feel tense, uncommunicative, or even hostile for the remainder of the interview period, with the result that the interviewer will find it difficult or impossible to get the information she needs.

A study conducted by the Survey Research Center bears out the importance of establishing a good relationship with the interviewee. It showed that, when individuals were questioned about a previous survey in which they had been interviewed, the highest percentage expressed their feelings about the interviewer and the process of the interview. Comparatively few reacted to the content of the survey. In other words, the relationship they established with the interviewer impressed the interviewees most.

The first job of the interviewer when the candidate appears is to create an atmosphere conducive to a free flow of factual information. To do this takes understanding, a feeling for the applicant, and a sense of knowing how and when to elicit responses. Techniques can be learned, but firsthand experience is essential. It is not enough to try to establish a relationship with a sophisticated applicant by flashing a smile, offering a cigarette, and making a remark about the weather.

Let's see how Tom Donovan, the marketing department head for a large firm, handles the introduction with his management training applicants. He realizes that the applicant has an important career decision hinging on the answers and the impressions he or she gives during this brief period and that this has probably caused some degree of anxiety to build up within the applicant.

Tom greets the applicant and introduces himself. He lets the applicant know what to call him during the interview, by saying, "Why don't you call me Tom?" He also asks the applicant what he prefers to be called. (An interviewer can unconsciously irritate the applicant throughout the interview by calling him by his given name, which appears on the application, without ever realizing that the applicant detests that name and prefers to be called by a nickname or a middle name.) If Tom is recruiting on a college campus, he also tells the candidate what company he represents, since students sometimes have several interviews scheduled at close intervals and tend to become confused. He always tells the applicant that he works in marketing. (It's a good idea to let the candidate know whether you represent the personnel department or a technical division, so that they have some idea whether you are an expert in their specialty area. Some applicants feel more comfortable if they know they are talking with one who shares their particular interests and represents the specific portion of the organization for which they are applying, rather than with an employment specialist who interviews candidates for positions throughout the organization.)

When he has taken care of these preliminaries, Tom usually takes a seat facing and near the applicant, which gets him out from behind his large desk. This gesture in itself can act as an icebreaker. He forces himself to relax both his voice and his posture. Rather than jumping right into the questioning, he may spend a few minutes exchanging pleasant small talk or conversing about something of mutual interest—perhaps a topic he has picked up from a clue on the application blank, such as a mutual acquaintance at XYZ Company or a mutual hobby. (Tom realizes, however, that in a few cases applicants may be very anxious to get right down to the business of the interview; in these cases, he respects the applicant's needs by making the introductory stage brief and beginning the assessment phase of the interview.)

There are few set guidelines for what works well during the opening moments of an interview. A remark about the weather or the offering of a cup of coffee, for instance, might seem very trite indeed to a sophisticated applicant who has attended dozens of interviews and has received the same opening treatment at each of them. On the other hand, it might be just the thing on a blustery day if handled in a sincere and friendly manner. The most important advice is to be natural, not phony.

During the opening stages of the interview, and during successive stages as well, the most important characteristics an interviewer can exhibit are permissiveness in regard to the expression of feelings, freedom from pressure and coercion, and, in the words of Carl Rogers, "warmth and responsiveness expressing itself in genuine interest in the client and acceptance of him as a person."

While Tom and the candidate are getting acquainted, Tom is watching for clues that will help him determine his approach to this particular applicant. He tries to be sensitive to signs that indicate the candidate's confidence level, his degree of reticence or willingness to volunteer information, any aggressiveness of hostility that may be present, and so on. He also tries to evaluate the level of the candidate's verbal fluency and language skills, so that he can structure his questions accordingly. He asks himself, "Is this individual going to be a reluctant communicator? Is he apt to be the type of person who will take over the interview and try to run it his way? Has he had some bad experiences that make him frightened or defensive, so that I have to proceed very slowly and gradually? Or is he sophisticated, experienced at interviewing, and self-assured? What kind of outlook and approach do I need with this individual? How much warming up does he need before I get into the heart of the questioning? Is he ready to go, or should I extend this introductory phase until he feels more comfortable?"

Tom can often get some clues as to the way the individual applicant might be expected to react even before he arrives by looking at his application blank or any other available data. He can guess at the individual's level of sophistication and his probable degree of confidence by taking a look at his educational level, the number of jobs he has held, the level at which he is seeking employment, whether or not he is currently employed, and so forth. These facts give him some feeling for the applicant's recent experiences and their possible effect on his willingness or ability to communicate. If a candidate is not a college graduate, for instance, and if he has held only one entry-level job and has been unemployed for several months, Tom might guess that this candidate could be relatively unsophisticated, under a great deal of stress to find employment, and thus rather uneasy or even defensive when he arrives for his interview. Of course, this guess could be a long way off target, and Tom will have to use the opening stages of the interview to determine this.

The introductory phase of the interview is very important in determining how things will go during the more intensive questioning phases, and the interviewer should use this preliminary stage to establish a permissive climate for communication. Too many interviewers fail in their initial efforts at establishing communication because they are too anxious to rush the applicant on toward the information-gathering stage or to delve into sensitive topics before the applicant is psychologically ready to communicate. Of course, it is possible with a very sophisticated or practiced applicant to spend too much time warming up or being so solicitous that it seems phony when the applicant is actually eager to get into the body of the interview. Even with the sophisticated candidate, though, questions or remarks which might seem too personal or insulting in the early portion of the interview are best left until later, when they could seem perfectly appropriate. The key is for the interviewer to assess the candidate's needs and his readiness to proceed and then to handle him accordingly.

While Tom is chatting with the candidate and assessing his verbal behavior, he is also watching for nonverbal signs that the candidate is ready to proceed. If Tom has been successful in establishing a comfortable relationship and putting the candidate at ease, the applicant will probably be speaking normally without undue signs of nervousness and will not exhibit any of the common nonverbal signs of anxiety discussed in Chapter 2, such as excessive perspiration or failure to establish eye contact. If these signs of anxiety are present, Tom extends the introductory portion of the interview somewhat, in order to improve the applicant's responsiveness and his own relationship with him.

Once Tom feels that the applicant has relaxed and is in a frame of mind that will facilitate communication on a deep level, he enters the "structure" phase of the interview. This is merely a sentence or two that will let the applicant know what to expect. What will be asked of him in the course of the interview? How will information be used, and is it to be kept confidential? Is he to report factual information only or communicate his own attitudes and feelings? Tom avoids being too specific in outlining the structure, in case he wants to change his plan as the interview progresses, but he tries, as the name of this phase implies, to structure the situation somewhat for the applicant.

Tom might say, for instance: "Pauline, I'd like to spend the first part of our interview asking you some questions about your background and interests, so we can get an idea of how you might fit into our management training program. Whatever you tell me will be used to help us determine this, but it won't be repeated to anyone outside our management team; so I hope you'll be absolutely candid in expressing your opinions and feelings about your work. After that, I'll be glad to answer any questions you might have about the training program or about the company in general."

The structure phase, then, lets Pauline know what she can expect; it implies permissiveness to speak honestly, and it tells her that she'll have a chance to ask her own questions later. If the interviewer intends to write down Pauline's responses during the interview, he should also let her know this and ask for her permission during this stage of the interview. (If he intends to tape the interview, he should ask permission at the very beginning of the introductory phase, to avoid being accused of invasion of privacy.) Like the introduction, the structure phase is designed to facilitate the free flow of communication by putting the candidate at ease and making her feel comfortable with the interviewer.

Only after these early stages have been concluded and the interviewer feels that he has established a satisfactory relationship with the interviewee and a climate conducive to meaningful communication, should he proceed to the information-gathering stage, which will be taken up in later chapters.

Chapter 6
The Cone System
of Interviewing

It is in the body of the interview, or the assessment phase, that the interviewer must gather the information she needs about the applicant in order to fulfill her objectives (i.e., to determine whether the applicant fits the job). If an interviewer has prepared adequately for the interview, she should already know what her objectives are and what types of specific information she needs to fulfill them. But many inexperienced interviewers falter at this stage of the interview because they don't know how to go about gathering these necessary bits of information. They are unsure how to approach the candidate with their questions.

FLEXIBLE VS. PATTERNED INTERVIEWING

Basically, there are two types of interviews, which are classified according to the way in which questions are asked and the way in which they are programmed into the interview. The first type is often called the "flexible interview." It is free and nondirective, permitting the applicant to express his or her experiences and interests with minimum direction on the part of the interviewer. An interviewer is using an extremely flexible approach if he begins the body of the interview with a question such as: "Why don't you tell me all about yourself and why you are interested in working for XYZ?" If the applicant faced with this question is relatively articulate, she may well spend the remainder of the allotted time in answering this question. Meanwhile, the interviewer will learn quite a lot about the candidate and what she considers to be the important or interesting facts about herself. But there are major drawbacks in the totally flexible approach: The candidate will obviously avoid talking about those portions of her background that she is not proud of; and, while she may tell the interviewer some very interesting things indeed, chances are they will not include all the things the interviewer needs to know in order to make a hiring decision or a recommendation. In other words, it is highly unlikely that a totally flexible interview will result in the attainment of all the objectives of the interviewer.

The approach at the opposite end of the scale is called the "patterned interview." In the completely patterned approach, the interviewer utilizes a printed form to provide comprehensive and orderly recording of data considered essential to the job. The questions that will be asked and even the order in which they will be asked are predetermined. The patterned interview does have some advantages. Everything is set on paper, so that the interviewer knows exactly what to ask. The procedure is standard; all applicants for the same job are asked the same questions even if several interviewers are interviewing for the same position. Finally, it is easy to provide a permanent record of the applicant's response, and this record can be compared later with those from other interviews.

The disadvantages of the patterned interview, on the other hand, are usually considered to outweigh the advantages of standardization and convenience. The process is too stereotyped, resulting in the loss of flexibility and spontaneity. The procedure often disintegrates into an interrogation, giving the applicant the feeling that he or she is being subjected to the "third degree." The interviewer is apt to take notes constantly throughout the interview. The interviewer doesn't really develop a feel for the personality of the applicant or for the emphasis he places on various aspects of his life and background. Furthermore, the interviewee doesn't get to know the interviewer, which could reduce the company's chance of hiring the best prospective employees.

In short, the patterned interview presents severe barriers to a good flow of communication, while the completely flexible interview reduces opportunities for the interviewer to obtain answers to all of his questions. Most interviewers, therefore, will have greater success with what we call a "nondirective guided approach." This approach is a compromise between the flexible and the patterned interview. It allows the interviewer an opportunity to program his objectives into the body of the interview through the use of a series of "cones," while still remaining flexible enough to give the applicant freedom to articulate the things he or she considers important.

THE CONE DEFINED

The cone system is the main tool utilized to implement the nondirective guided approach to interviewing. It allows the interviewer to meet his or her objectives by programming them into a series of cones that make up the body of the interview.

A cone could be considered a "mini-interview" or one of a series of interviews within the interview. It covers one broad area of investigation that will help the interviewer meet his objectives, and it allows the interviewer to cover the subject systematically by beginning with a broad general question and building on the information obtained from the applicant's response. The interviewer proceeds from this initial question and response, which are flexible in nature, to very specific questions that allow him to dig out the details he needs to know about the candidate. By setting up a series of cones to investigate various aspects of the candidate's background, the interviewer can program into the interview the topics he needs to cover to meet all his objectives.

A cone can be run in any number of subject areas. In selecting his cones, the interviewer will be guided by the available background information on the applicant, which might suggest a wide variety of possible cones, and by his own major objectives for the interview, which will suggest which of the available cones might prove most lucrative for obtaining the specific types of information desired. Some of the most popularly used cones concern previous employment, educational background, special training, outside activities and interests, and attitudes and motivations.

When an applicant has a past employment record, at least one cone, and frequently more than one, will be run on this subject. Generally, each previous job would constitute a separate cone topic; that is, if a cone were run on the candidate's most recent job, the interviewer would begin a new cone if he also wanted to explore the candidate's next-to-last job. An exception might be made for the young applicant who has had only a series of relatively insignificant part-time or summer jobs, in which case these might well be lumped together for exploration in one cone. The interviewer might begin such a cone by asking: "I see you've had several summer jobs during your school years. Could you tell me a little about them?"

Several separate cones dealing with educational background also suggest themselves, depending upon the candidate. For the applicant with a recent graduate degree, the interviewer would probably want to run one cone on graduate education and perhaps another on undergraduate education. Most interviewers feel there is little to be gained by running a cone on high-school education, unless the applicant has just recently graduated from high school and is applying for an entry-level position. College graduates or postgraduates have often forgotten many of their high-school experiences and tend to place little importance on their accomplishments during their years there.

Special training, such as military experience or Peace Corps or Job Corps service, also provides cone topics which may contain a wealth of information. For many years, the discussion of military service during the interview was unpopular among interviewers; now, however, many effective interviewers realize that applicants may have gained valuable training in technical or leadership skills through military service or in related campus programs such as ROTC. Often, these experiences and skills and related attitudes are not revealed during the course of the interview unless a cone is run specifically on military service.

Cones on outside activities and interests may cover a wide realm of topics. These may be lumped together in one broad "outside interest" cone, or the interviewer may select one activity that interests him from the application blank and run a cone on just that one activity.

Generally, the attitudes and motivations of the applicant will be ascertained or inferred from information he volunteers during cones on some of the above subjects rather than from a separate cone designed to deal specifically with attitudes or motivations. However, it is possible to set up a cone for the specific purpose of exploring an attitude. Such a cone might begin, for example, with the following question: "Would you tell me a little about your career goals and what kinds of things you are looking for in a job?"

Finally, an interviewer might want to leave time for a miscellaneous cone, in which he collects and examines a number of "keys" or "flags" that were picked up in other cones. (Later in this chapter, keys and flags will be explained in greater detail.) For instance, if previous cones have yielded the information that the applicant quit every major undertaking he began after three or four months, the interviewer might well run a final cone to try to uncover the cause of this pattern.

This list of possible cone topics is by no means all-inclusive. An adept interviewer who has carefully charted his objectives might well select other topics for cones—for instance, "geographic preference," for a job that requires relocation. But the topics discussed above are certainly those most commonly selected for structuring cones in the selection interview situation.

As shown in Figure 6.1, the cone takes its shape from the types of questions that are posed during each portion of it. At the top of the cone, or the beginning of each cone in the interview situation, the interviewer uses very broad or open-focus questions. As the cone narrows, the question focus narrows as well, so that the interviewer will introduce very specific, closed-focus questions at the bottom.

The communication cone which we are using here differs in one important respect from an actual cone-shaped container in which we might, for instance, pour a liquid. In the interview type of cone, our purpose is not to drive the applicant directly to the bottom of the

Figure 6.1   The Cone

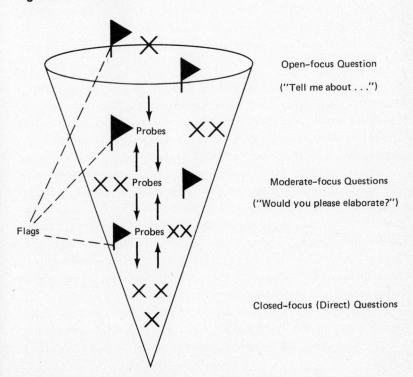

Open–focus Question
("Tell me about . . .")

Moderate–focus Questions
("Would you please elaborate?")

Closed–focus (Direct) Questions

cone first but to keep him or her moving within the cone until we have gained the information we need about this particular topic. As the arrows in Figure 6.1 indicate, communication, unlike liquids, can go both up and down the cone. Communication can also travel around the cone, remaining at one level for quite a while before moving up or down. Pushing the candidate to the bottom of the cone should be avoided until it becomes imperative.

USE OF QUESTION FOCUS

The Open-Focus Question

Let's examine the open-focus question that is used to begin each cone. This is a question that is quite nondirective. It simply specifies the broad area that the interviewer wishes to investigate, without telling the candidate what he or she is expected to say about that topic. Some examples of open-focus questions are:

> Could you describe your first job with the Ford Motor Company for me?
>
> I noticed that you went to the University of Michigan. Would you tell me about your education there?
>
> You apparently are involved in a number of outside activities. Would you discuss some of them for me?
>
> I noticed you spent some time in the Air Force. Would you take me through some of your Air Force experiences?

The reader will notice that all these questions just open up a topic at the top of the cone. They are very broad, designed to get the applicant talking and to give him a chance to say what he feels is important about the subject. One of the tests of an open-focus question is that you can't answer it with "Yes," "No," or a brief sentence or phrase. Another is that it does not suggest to the applicant what specific kinds of information the interviewer wants. It does not suggest what aspects of the general topic the interviewer considers important, nor does it imply any answer that will be considered "correct" by the interviewer. In other words, at the top of the cone, the applicant is made to feel that the interviewer has selected a broad subject, and anything the applicant wishes to say about that subject will be acceptable and of interest to the interviewer.

One word of warning is in order: It is possible to make open-focus questions too open for the applicant to handle comfortably. Some open-focus questions are just too broad in scope. A typical example is "Tell me about yourself." Others that may be too broad are those that require the individual to summarize many, many years' activities, such as "Describe your educational background," when addressed to a person who is a postdoctoral candidate, or "Take me through your work experience," addressed to the candidate who has had 20 years of experience in industry. Questions of this magnitude could be confusing to some applicants; they are not considered good communication. And even if the applicant can handle the question, it can be terribly time-consuming. It is a good idea to moderate such broad questions somewhat. (Example: Change "Describe your educational background" to "Describe your educational experiences while you were working toward your Ph.D.") This is still an open-focus question, but it gives the candidate some boundaries within which to operate and helps him to structure his comments more effectively.

The Moderate-Focus Question

The middle of the cone comprises moderate-focus questions. At this point, the shape of the cone is narrowing, but it is not yet tight and closed, as it will be at the very bottom. The moderate-focus question, then, is narrower in scope than the open-focus question at the top, but it is not a closed or direct question. It still cannot be answered tersely or with a "Yes" or "No."

A moderate-focus question will depend upon the open-focus question that preceded it at the beginning of the cone and will also depend upon the information already volunteered by the applicant. This is one of the tests of a moderate-focus question; it must pertain to something the applicant has already said. Although an open-focus or a direct-focus question can be asked of a person who has not yet said a word, a moderate-focus question makes no sense except in the context of the respondent's previous statements.

Let's consider an example to illustrate the way in which the moderate-focus question is dependent upon the preceding open-focus question and upon previously volunteered information. In a particular interview, the first cone might be started with the following question: "John, would you fill me in on your experience with Collins Radio as an engineer?" After John has volunteered some information in response to this question, the interviewer might well ask: "You say you were a supervisor in the avionics division of the flight research group for a while. Would you tell me more specifically what your duties were there?" This is a moderate-focus question because it pinpoints a more specific area of the topic initiated by the open-focus question; it is based on information John has already offered (the fact that he was a supervisor in a particular division), and it would be pointless to ask such a question except in the light of information already volunteered by John. Although it is narrower in focus than the open-focus question, it avoids the specificity of a direct, or closed-focus, question, because it is still too broad to be answered tersely or with a simple negative or affirmative.

Most of the communication in the interview takes place in the middle of the cone, during moderate-focus questioning. It is here that the interviewer can probe most successfully by skillfully leading the conversation so that the applicant tells him what he needs to know in order to meet his objectives yet at the same time avoiding rapid-fired, abrupt questions that can make the applicant uncomfortable or defensive. The art of probing to meet objectives will be discussed more thoroughly later in this chapter and also in the next.

The Closed-Focus Question

At the bottom of the cone, it may be necessary to use some closed-focus or direct-focus questions. A closed-focus question is any kind of question that can be fully answered with "Yes," "No," or a very brief sentence or phrase. Examples of direct questions are:

Where did you go to school?
Was that first job a full-time job?
Your only outside activity is skiing?
Was your graduate degree in English or history?
What was your rank when you left the Navy?

Direct questions are not considered to contribute to good communication, although they may be necessary in order to get the last bits of information from the applicant if he cannot be enticed to volunteer the necessary facts through the use of moderate-focus questions. Whereas an open-focus or a moderate-focus question is considered to be nonthreatening, in that it gives the respondent some leeway in framing his response, the direct or closed-focus question is often perceived as threatening because it pins the respondent down to very specific information. If the applicant doesn't know the answer, or if he is very sensitive about the answer or if he feels that it will reflect poorly upon him, resistance occurs in the bottom of the cone. Closed-focus questions, especially if they are fired at the applicant in rapid succession, are often perceived as a form of interrogation or a means of extracting information that the applicant may be trying to withhold. Finally, even if the applicant does not feel threatened or become defensive, he is unlikely to volunteer any extraneous information in response to direct questioning, with the result that the interviewer who concentrates mainly on closed-focus questions will miss the opportunity to uncover many important clues to the applicant's background, personality, and attitudes.

For these reasons, skilled interviewers attempt to stay out of the bottom of the cone unless it is absolutely necessary for them to ask direct questions in order to obtain the factual information necessary to meet their objectives. After a little practice and experience with the cone system, most interviewers find they are able to get out of the bottom of the cone, once they have asked a direct question or two, by using a moderate-focus probe to push the applicant back up the cone. This technique can be explained more clearly later in the chapter, when we have discussed the use of probes. These are a special type of moderate-focus question.

FLAGS

An important feature of the cone system is what we call "flags" or "keys." A flag is a clue that the interviewer picks up from what the applicant is saying (or what he is *not* saying). It may be any statement or word or the avoidance of a particular subject that alerts the interviewer to explore this aspect of the topic at hand more thoroughly. Flags may come in different "colors," or meanings. If the interviewer picks up a clue which has a positive association with the needs of the job, we call this clue a "green" flag or a "plus." On the other hand, a flag having a negative connotation in relationship to the job can be a "minus," or a "red" flag. Notice the importance here of having the job requirements firmly in mind: Without this basis for comparison, the interviewer may well pick up a flag, but he will be unable to determine whether it is a plus or a minus factor. In other words, flags cannot be designated "red" or "green" except in relation to the job requirements.

Many interviewers, who otherwise use the cone system very well, miss a great deal of pertinent information offered to them by the applicant because they fail to identify flags. Often, this happens because the interviewer simply isn't listening carefully. On other occasions, he may hear the flag but dismiss it as unimportant information rather than perceive it as a key to some aspect of the candidate's background or personality which could lead to the correct decision about his or her suitability for the job.

Probably the best way to illustrate the nature of flags and their importance in the interview is to examine some examples taken from actual interviews. In the first, an interviewer is talking to an applicant about a data processing job which, at certain times of the year, requires a lot of overtime. The applicant mentions that his outside activities require him to attend meetings almost every evening. An interviewer who is only half listening might miss this flag, obvious as it may seem to the reader; he might well say to himself, "Well, he must be a good, civic-minded fellow to devote so much time to these worthwhile activities." But in dismissing the applicant's remark, he would be missing a red flag. The astute interviewer would want to delve more deeply into this subject, to determine whether the applicant would stick with the job when it began to interfere with his many outside activities or whether he would be likely to resign in favor of a position that did not require overtime.

In another instance, the interviewer might be talking with a person who has a very outstanding typing speed, according to her typing tests. The interviewer, who is very impressed with this applicant's skills, is considering hiring her for a position that requires extensive typing of statistics. If, during the interview, the applicant says she resigned from her last job because the kinds of typing she did were not challenging or interesting to her, the interviewer has a flag. We know it is a flag, but at this point, it is impossible to determine whether it is a red or a green flag. Before it can be assigned a color, or a plus or minus connotation, the interviewer will have to follow up by finding out what kinds of typing she found distasteful. If it turns out that her last job mostly involved typing numbers, then chances are she won't like a new statistical typing job any better, even if she is the best-qualified applicant in terms of typing skill. That, then, would be a red flag in relation to this particular position. But if her last job consisted primarily of typing form letters, then her statement about her feelings could be a green flag; perhaps statistical work could be very challenging and satisfying to her. The interviewer who is so impressed with the candidate's typing speed that he is not listening alertly for flags could miss this clue altogether, and hire the woman for a specific typing job without any indication as to whether she wishes to use her skills in this particular way.

It should be pointed out here that by picking up flags a good interviewer will often learn things that the candidate had no intention of telling him. In the two preceding examples, for instance, the applicants might well have disguised their true feelings in response to a direct question. They might, in fact, have been unable to analyze their actual attitudes even if they had wanted to be truthful. The data processing applicant, for instance, might well believe that he wants the job badly enough to give up some of his outside activities, although careful questioning could reveal that this would present him with a dilemma which would make him very unhappy and could well lead to his early resignation from the position. By the same token, the secretarial candidate may know very well that she hates typing statistics and that the position for which she is being interviewed would be boring, but she may be trying to get the position anyway because she needs the money badly and this job pays better than others that are available. Perhaps she believes that she can do the job well whether she likes it or not, or perhaps she plans to stay on the job only until she is able to find one which is more to her liking. In either case, since she wants the statistical typing job, at least for the present, she is surely not going to volunteer to the interviewer the fact that she intensely dislikes typing numbers. He will have to pick this up by following up when she hints at her dissatisfaction with her previous assignment.

Another form of flag may be picked up when an applicant seems to be purposely avoiding a particular subject. Perhaps she tries to evade the question or answers the question but omits some important aspect. For example, a young woman, in discussing her college education, may describe her freshman year enthusiastically and then jump to a detailed description of her senior year. This absence of any mention of the two intervening years should serve as a flag to the interviewer: What happened during those two years that makes the applicant pass over them without mention? In this case, the flag exists in what the applicant did *not* say, rather than in what she actually said.

Of course, not all flags represent information that the applicant is trying to disguise or withhold. Often, especially in the case of green flags, or plus factors, they may simply signify something that the candidate has forgotten to mention or that she considers unimportant or unrelated to the job, unless probed for further details. For instance, if a candidate says she "enjoyed" serving as president of her college drama club, the interviewer who follows up this flag may find that the very characteristics which made her enjoy this experience are the traits that would be definite plusses in the position available with his company. Certainly the applicant did not mean to withhold this information; perhaps she was just reticent to mention these strong points until she was asked about them specifically, or perhaps she did not perceive their relevance to the position for which she was applying.

So far, the flags we have discussed have been picked up during the actual interview from the applicant's responses to questions within the cone. However, flags may also show up outside the cone proper. The interviewer may notice, for instance, that the application does not account for a two-year interval between the applicant's first job and his second job. He would want to pick up this clue and probe during the interview to find out where the applicant was and what he was doing during the unaccounted for period.

In general, then, flags or keys are clues which tell the interviewer that he needs to follow up on a particular line of information, to find out how people feel about their backgrounds, about using their skills and meeting their commitments, and about themselves. Flags must be picked up through careful listening and pursued in a nondirective way.

PROBING FOR LATENT CONTENT

The probe is the interviewer's primary tool for encouraging the applicant to communicate with him on a level that goes beyond the superficial. It is used to elicit further information from the applicant without giving him the impression that he is being interrogated.

Probes fall into the category of moderate-focus questions; their structure depends upon what has gone before; and they cannot be answered tersely. An effective probe technique must enable the interviewer to motivate additional communication; it must enhance or maintain the interpersonal relationship that has already been established, and it must not introduce bias or modify the meaning of the primary question. Proper probe questions create additional understanding between the two individuals. They let the applicant know the interviewer is interested and has comprehended what the applicant has said so far and serve to encourage the interviewee to explain himself more completely and candidly.

"Magic Words"

Since effective probes must not reflect the interviewer's bias or modify the meaning of the original question, the most useful probes are neutral phrases. Some interviewers like to remember what they call the three "magic words": *describe, expand,* and *elaborate.* They are referred to as magic words because of their almost magical ability to elicit further information from the applicant. Some examples of probes that utilize these magic words, or phrases that are similar in effect, are:

How do you mean?
I'd like to know more of your thinking on that.
I'm not sure what you have in mind.
Why do you feel that way?
Could you elaborate on that?
Would you fill me in on that?
Would you describe that in more detail?
Do you have any other reasons for feeling that way?

These probes all have several things in common. They show the applicant that the interviewer is listening and is interested in what he is saying; they do not indicate to the applicant that the interviewer either approves or disapproves of what he has said; and they cannot be answered tersely by the candidate—he must pursue the subject further.

The Pregnant Pause and the Assertive Phrase

There are other, related techniques that experienced interviewers utilize to supplement the primary question. Some of the most useful and common are also the simplest. One such technique is for the interviewer to say nothing at all when the applicant pauses, so that the applicant feels compelled to continue. This technique, often called the "pregnant pause," is one of the most effective ways of encouraging further communication. Many interviewers seem to feel they must fill every silence by jumping in immediately with another question. By doing so, they are missing comments that would very likely be forthcoming from the candidate after a slight pause.

Another related technique is the interviewer's provision of a brief assertion of his understanding and interest, such as "I see" or "um-hm." Such phrases, sometimes accompanied by a nod of the head, tell the applicant that he is communicating and is understood but that he has not yet given a complete response to the question.

In the following conversation, an interviewer utilizes a combination of these probing techniques to elicit information from a rather reticent candidate:

INT.: You say you'd like to work for our company. What kind of work would you like?

App.: Well, I'm not sure. (*Pause.*) I was thinking of something in accounting.

Int.: I see.

App.: I think so. I took some accounting in business school. (*Pause.*) In my job at ABC Company, I worked as a records clerk.

Int.: Could you tell me more specifically what you did?

App.: Well, first I just did the routine record-keeping—payroll, invoices, and so on. But later the president of the company had me assigned to some special research projects, and that was a lot more interesting.

Int.: Would you elaborate on that?

The Summary Probe

Another nondirective technique that some interviewers use with great success is called the "summary" technique. Here, the interviewer explores the subject in greater depth by summarizing or reflecting what the candidate has just told her. This technique conveys permissiveness and acceptance as well as invites further communication, and it lets the applicant hear succinctly from the interviewer what he is communicating. The applicant thus has a chance to make modifications in what he has communicated if he feels that the interviewer's reflections do not accurately represent the meaning he hopes to convey. This technique is especially useful with fairly inarticulate candidates when the interviewer herself is not absolutely certain that she has understood correctly, but its usefulness is by no means limited to this situation. A conversation in which the interviewer relies heavily on this technique might sound like this:

Int.: What kind of work are you doing on your present job? Let's see, that's with the Bland Company, isn't it?

App.: Yeah, I've been there for two years and I'm fed up.

Int.: You're anxious to leave them.

App.: I sure am. I'm the youngest person there, and I get all the junk to do that nobody else wants.

Int.: You get the dregs, eh?

App.: I really do. I didn't mind at first, but I think now I can do much more than I have a chance to do there.

Int.: Tell me what you have in mind.

App.: Well, for one thing, I don't get a chance to use my shorthand. I don't take more than one letter a week. Most of my work is just typing reports with hundreds of tables and charts.

INT.: You'd like to get away from typing statistics.

APP.: Oh, I don't mind typing numbers. I'm pretty good at it, and I enjoy it. But I think I could do some other things besides—more challenging things.

INT.: You feel you can do higher-level work.

APP.: I sure'do. I went to business school to be a secretary, and on my present job I don't have a chance.

INT.: You'd like a secretarial job with more shorthand, is that it?

APP.: Yes, I would. Do you have any secretarial openings?

There are certain drawbacks to the summary probe technique in the hands of an unskilled interviewer. One is the inadvertent inclusion of the interviewer's opinion in the summary statement. Often, an applicant will recognize that this opinion has been included but will accept the statement rather than deny the correctness of the interpretation in order to avoid contradicting the interviewer. Another danger is the possible presentation of the summary probe in a way that is unacceptable to the applicant or that reflects the applicant in an unfavorable light. Even if this type of summary is technically correct, it may well elicit a defensive reaction and thus a digression from the applicant.

Variation of Probes

Since the effective interviewer will use a large number of probes during the course of an interview, she will want to master all or most of the various probing techniques—"magic words," the pregnant pause, the brief assertion of understanding, and the summary probe—and to use them interchangeably to provide variety. Any one of the techniques, if used exclusively, can rapidly become so repetitive and predictable to the applicant that it discourages, rather than encourages, further in-depth communication.

DURATION AND DEPTH OF CONES

The cone system, in addition to allowing the interviewer to plan his objectives into the interview, is also a useful means of allocating time during the interview. For a half-hour interview, with roughly 15 minutes in the body of the interview for the pursual of information, three 5-minute cones could very easily be programmed in. A 5-minute cone should contain between 8 and 12 questions as a rule, with most of these being moderate-focus questions in the middle of the cone or probes from lower down to follow up on flags that have been picked up by the interviewer. With most candidates, fewer questions will fail to achieve enough depth, and a much greater number of questions will not leave time for the candidate to respond adequately to each one. Sometimes, too, an interviewer who regularly asks 20 or more questions within a 5-minute cone will find that he has resorted primarily to direct, or closed-focus, questioning.

Of course, the optimum number of questions for a 5-minute cone will vary somewhat with the verbosity and articulateness of the candidate. The interviewer may find that he has to use more than 12 with the extremely shy interviewee and perhaps only four or five with the gregarious candiate—especially if the latter happens to include in his initial response most of the information the interviewer hoped to obtain through probing. But for the average candidate, 8–12 questions per 5-minute cone is a good rule of thumb, and the interviewer who deviates consistently from this formula would do well to examine his probing technique. He may be committing errors that restrict the flow of communication or keep it from reaching the necessary depth.

Many interviewers, when they first begin to use the cone system of interviewing, make the mistake of trying to run too many cones in the amount of time available. If the applicant has held six previous jobs, the inexperienced interviewer may attempt to run a separate cone on each of these—plus, perhaps, another on his military career, one on his college education, and one on his outside activities. In an interview with 15 minutes set aside for the body, only a little over a minute and a half could be devoted to each of these nine cones. This would prove a futile exercise; the cones would be so brief that only superficial information could be obtained from each. It is much more effective in an interview of this length to set up fewer cones—those that would appear from the application data submitted to be most lucrative in terms of information relating to the job requirements—and to utilize probes within these cones to get at the main objectives of the interview.

Of course, in an in-depth or hiring-decision interview for a professional applicant where time is less limited, the interviewer might well run a greater number of cones, and he is more likely to have enough time flexibility to stay in a given cone for a longer period of time if it is still yielding relevant information.

BRIDGING

Once an interviewer has remained in a cone for five minutes or so and is satisfied that he has exhausted the content of that particular topic, he must move on to the next cone he has planned. To make this transition, he uses a bridge between the cones. Bridging is a very important part of the cone system, because it provides separation and definition between the cones. It is not a complicated process but simply a means of getting out of one cone and into another in such a way that the applicant realizes that a major topic switch is taking place.

An example of a satisfactory bridge is: "John, I think I have a pretty good understanding of what you did at the University of Alabama. Now, I wonder if we could move over and talk about your first job with the Southern Corporation. Would you tell me about that?" The interviewer has closed one cone, moved over, and started the second cone with an open-focus question, so that the applicant feels he has satisfactorily completed his explanation of one topic and knows exactly what he is supposed to talk about next. Without this sort of bridge, the applicant who is very involved in explaining his activities and feelings at one stage of his life may very well be confused and disoriented by a sudden open-focus question on an unrelated topic.

PROBLEMS IN CONES

Like most interviewing techniques, the cone system will fail to yield the necessary information if the cones are improperly handled. Some of the common problems that cause the system to fall short of expectations in the hands of inexperienced interviewers are discussed below, along with the solutions to these problems.

Improper Question Focus

Many interviewers try to operate the cone system without a complete understanding of question focus. The most common error is the attempt to open a cone with a closed-focus question, such as "Where have you worked previously?" When the applicant responds with the names of two or three companies, the unskilled interviewer finds himself forced into an interrogative role right from the outset; he sees no alternative to asking a series of direct or closed-focus questions. Another common error is the use of direct questions in the belief that they are moderate-focus probes. Often, the difference is to be found in the way the question is worded rather than in the basic content of the question. If, for example, a candidate has mentioned that she worked for the Barnaby Trucking Company, the interviewer might ask: "What did you do there?" If so, the applicant can appropriately answer, "I worked in the office." She has been asked and has responded to a direct question. But if the interviewer rewords the question, asking "Would you elaborate on your duties there?", he has changed the question into a moderate-focus probe. The applicant will feel obligated to provide much more extensive and helpful information than she supplied in response to the direct question.

To use the cone system properly, then, it is necessary to begin with an open-focus question and to use moderate-focus probes in preference to direct questions whenever possible. Each interviewer who uses the cone system should review the subject of question focus periodically, to ensure that he understands the proper way to open the cone and keep it moving.

Incidentally, many interviewers fall into the trap of believing they have asked the right kind of question simply because they received the right kind of answer. It is possible, of course, that an interviewer can attempt to open a cone with a direct question ("Where have you worked previously?") and receive a detailed answer from the candidate that outlines where he worked, what his duties were, how he felt about them—in short, all the information the interviewer could have hoped for had he begun with an open-focus question. Unfortunately, however, most candidates are not gregarious or comfortable enough to carry the interviewer in spite of his mistakes; the vast majority take questions literally and answer just what is asked, without venturing to volunteer further information. The wise interviewer, then, will not rely on the eventuality that a closed-focus question *could* be answered with a wealth of information; he will focus his questions so that they *must* be answered with the thoroughness and detail he intends.

Getting Trapped at the Bottom

It would be comforting to be able to report that once a cone has been properly opened with an open-focus question all will be well, and information will gush forth at a gratifying rate. Unfortunately, not all applicants have been coached in the subject of question focus, and many an interviewer has found that his open-focus question has been destroyed by a few ill-chosen words on the part of the applicant.

For example, the interviewer might begin with a perfectly proper open-focus question: "Could you tell me about your education at the University of Michigan?" Suppose the applicant counters with: "What do you want to know?" At this point, the inexperienced interviewer may well say, in desperation, "What did you major in?" This, of course, is a direct question. If the candidate answers it tersely, as he surely will, the interviewer is likely to resort to several more direct questions. He is stuck in the bottom of the cone.

In another situation, the interviewer might ask, "Would you discuss your military experience for me?" Suppose the applicant says: "Oh, there was really nothing to it. I served in the Army. I was in Germany for three years, and then I was discharged." If the interviewer comes back with a question such as "What did you think of your experience in the military?", the applicant can simply say, "I didn't like it," and the candidate has the interviewer in the bottom of the cone.

When communications break down in this way, the inexperienced interviewer finds himself stuck in the bottom of the cone, and he frequently can't get out. He doesn't want to conclude the cone, since he hasn't yet achieved his objectives within this cone; he doesn't want to remain at the bottom, asking a series of direct questions, because this constitutes poor communication and tends to place stress on the candidate; but he doesn't know how to get back up into the middle of the cone where meaningful communication can take place.

The answer to this dilemma is the use of moderate-focus probes—especially those "magic words" *expand, elaborate,* and *describe.* It will be almost impossible for the applicant to respond to these probes without offering some further information that will keep the cone going. So the probes move the applicant right back up to the middle of the cone and keep him communicating.

Let's take the two examples above, in which the unskilled interviewer found himself stuck in the bottom of the cone before he had hardly begun. In the first, in which he asks about the applicant's education and she counters with "What did you want to know?", he might say: "Describe your educational experiences at the University for me," or "Tell me anything you wish about the experiences you had there." Either of these moderate-focus probes should serve to push the candidate right back up the cone and gently force her to talk.

In the other situation, the candidate has answered the query about his military experience in a way but only with one or two sentences. In this case, the interviewer might say: "Could you please elaborate on some of the experiences you had as a soldier?" There again, he is employing a moderate-focus probe to steer the applicant right back up into the cone.

In both examples, the interviewer has used a moderate-focus probe to avoid a direct question during the early stages of the cone. By so doing, he has also avoided becoming trapped in the bottom of the cone before he has had a chance to explore the more lucrative types of information at the top and in the middle.

Changing the Subject

Frequently, an applicant will attempt to change the topic and move out of the cone into another area. This may be intentional (if the applicant does not want to discuss the selected topic for some reason), or it may simply be that the applicant's train of thought has led him farther and farther astray from the original question. In either case, the interviewer must exercise control and bring the candidate back into the cone. This can be done through a statement such as: "Well, I'd like to hear more about your outside activities later, but if you don't mind, let's back up right now and talk more about your graduate education at the University of Wisconsin." The interviewer must politely but firmly let the applicant know that he is interested in what the latter has to say and will provide an opportunity for him to say it later, but he has no intention of dropping the original subject at this point. It is essential that the interviewer keep the interviewee in the cone until he has exhausted, to his satisfaction, the areas of inquiry that he has programmed and planned into the cone.

Later, however, the interviewer should pursue the topic that the applicant apparently wanted to talk about, even if there is time to go into it only briefly. This serves two purposes: it reassures the candidate that the interviewer was, indeed, sincere when he expressed interest in the subject earlier; and it may yield some valuable information, since it is apparently a topic of great interest or importance to the candidate and one that he or she is willing to discuss.

The Chronology Obsession

In using the cone system (and any other interviewing system as well), some interviewers become so preoccupied with the chronology of the applicant's background that they miss out on quite a lot of information that would prove more valuable to them in the long run. They seem to have a compulsion to determine exactly when and in what order various experiences in the candidate's background took place. Some even interrupt the candidate at regular intervals while he is relating some experience or attitude with questions about the chronology: "When did you do that?", or "Was that before or after you worked in the grocery store?"

Of course, it is helpful to have some idea of the chronology of events, but generally this will be supplied in sufficient detail on the application blank or resumé. If it is not, find out these dates early in the interview and then forget about them and concentrate on the more interesting details of the applicant's experiences and attitudes.

There are at least two important reasons for abandoning the strictly chronological approach to interviewing. The first is that, quite often, the most recent experiences of the candidate are the ones that are of most interest to the interviewer and that are most closely related to the present job opening. Yet the interviewer who insists on "beginning at the beginning" and proceeding through the interview chronologically—high school, college, first job, second job, and so forth—may well run out of time before he ever arrives at the most recent and most informative stages of the applicant's background.

The second argument against the chronological compulsion is the danger that the candidate will become similarly obsessed during the course of the interview. Once he or she realizes that the interviewer places a great deal of emphasis on having events described in their proper order, the candidate will conscientiously try to please by relating them in this sequence. For some candidates, especially those with an extensive and varied background, this is such a difficult task that they begin to concentrate almost solely on the chronology of events. As a result, their descriptions of their actual experiences and feelings suffer from a lack of attention. Then, too, a chronological recitation of events tends to become a monotonous litany ("First I did so-and-so; then I went to such-and-such; then I . . ."). The danger here is that no one event or experience is given any more emphasis by the candidate than any other event or experience, and so the interviewer will be unable to interpret through tone or emphasis which experiences the candidate considered exciting, dull, important, or insignificant.

Leading Questions

Quite a few interviewers fall into the trap of asking leading questions in an effort to soften or avoid direct questions. Actually, leading questions are still direct questions, with the added disadvantage of suggesting the "correct" answer to the applicant. For instance, if the interviewer asks, "Did you enjoy your last job?", the applicant will often say "Yes" because he or she believes that this is the response the interviewer wants. On the other hand, if the interviewer asks, "How did you feel about your last job?", the applicant is more likely to express his own feelings because he has no way of knowing what answer will meet with approval.

Interviewers also attempt to avoid leading questions by asking a sort of "multiple-choice" leading question. This might be something like the following: "Which were your favorite courses—math, physical science, or statistics?" It is possible that none of the alternatives offered by the interviewer is correct; perhaps the candidate really liked his art classes better than any of the interviewer's alternatives. But he or she will tend to select one of the alternatives provided in the question, since those seem to be the answers that the interviewer will consider acceptable. Also, if several alternatives are offered in the question, candidates tend to become confused; the question cannot be mentally processed rapidly enough. The pitfalls of the multiple-choice leading question can be avoided by simply rephrasing the question: "Of all your courses, which did you like most?"

Superficial Planning

Too many interviewers feel that they have sufficiently planned the body of their interview once they have selected three or four areas in which they plan to run cones. On the contrary, it is essential that the interviewer learn to plan areas *within* each cone that he or she plans to explore in depth, rather than just select the general topic for each cone. These specific areas of investigation within the cone are the areas that will yield information relevant to the needs of the specific job opening.

In other words, it is not enough to decide that you will run a cone on the applicant's most recent position, which happened to be as manager of a division of the Ford Motor Company. No matter what position you were to interview this particular applicant for, you would probably run a cone on her most recent job. Now you must go a step further. What, specifically, do you need to find out about this most recent job that will help you decide whether the applicant meets the needs of the specific position for which you are interviewing her? You may decide, for example, that you need to find out in the course of this cone some of the following: the applicant's responsibilities; how many assets she controlled; how many people she managed; what techniques she used in managing people; how she felt about managing; what skills she brought to bear on the job; what skills she has that she felt were not used to their maximum potential on the job; what kinds of relationships she had with her peers, her subordinates, and the company in general; and her overall feelings about the job. These, then, would be your target areas during this particular cone. Only when they have been planned into the cone can you assume that you have planned at the level which will help you to meet your objectives for the interview.

Chapter 7
Applicant
Evaluation

The questions that usually loom largest in interviewers' minds are: How do I evaluate a candidate? How can I make a meaningful decision after only a very brief encounter as to this individiual's suitability for our position?

As we have mentioned in earlier chapters, the key to effective evaluation is prior planning. All too often interviewers conduct an interview without any particular "game plan," and only when the applicant has been dismissed do they begin to wonder how to evaluate him or her. This haphazard procedure can only lead to very vague and often completely erroneous conclusions about the candidate. An interviewer has failed if the most profound evaluative statement he can make at the end of an hour's interview is: "He seems to be a nice guy," or "She impressed me as very intelligent." Yet these are exactly the types of conclusions to which the interviewer will be limited unless he builds evaluative tools and techniques right into the body of his interview.

Even when the interview is well planned and well executed with the interviewer doing all the proper things, it is possible to evaluate the candidate incorrectly and to have the hiring decision rebound on you. Evaluation is probably the most difficult dimension of the art of interviewing, because of the many variables involved.

However, research done in the late 1960s and early 1970s has given us a better understanding of how we can turn some of these variables into constants in order to make more effective hiring decisions. Among the results of this research was the finding that interviewers' evaluations lack consistency. One interviewer may rate a candidate extremely high on a particular characteristic, such as maturity, and another may rate him or her extremely low on the same trait. In addition, a given interviewer may fluctuate widely from interview to interview in the types of behavior that he or she considers manifestations or indicators of a particular trait. We have attempted to mold several safeguards against this lack of consistency into our communication and evaluation systems, to enhance our batting average. Some of these safeguards, or techniques, are closely related to averaging or "hedging our bets" in this difficult assessment situation. These averaging techniques still do not assure us that our evaluation will be right, but they improve our chances of being correct, much as the technique of averaging improves our chances in the stock market.

Other techniques involve careful definition and consistent application of the characteristics we are looking for, so that interviewers can apply the same definition of a characteristic to every candidate they interview or to every relevant statement that a particular candidate makes. We have touched upon the need to define desirable characteristics in Chapter 4, and later in this chapter we will deal with specific indicators of various traits in an individual.

THE APPLICANT VS. THE JOB

What, precisely, should be evaluated? We have already discussed the need for matching the applicant to the job and the closeness of his or her match is what the interviewer must evaluate. Although an interviewer will naturally form some general impressions of the candidate's characteristics, these impressions are meaningless for evaluative purposes unless they can be directly related to the job requirements. In fact, very few characteristics can be judged either desirable or undesirable except as they relate to the position under consideration. (Is an exceedingly low level of energy and drive an undesirable characteristic? Certainly—for a salesperson! But it may be an absolutely necessary characteristic for a night watchman, who would very likely resign from boredom within a week if he were hyperactive and overly ambitious.)

Of course, a few interviewers are in the enviable position of having so many openings or such a flexible organization that they can at least partially tailor the job to fit the applicant. Most, however, do not enjoy this luxury. The general rule, then, is that an applicant cannot be judged "good" or "bad" except in relation to the specific requirements of the position for which he or she is being considered, and it is around these requirements that the evaluation process must be structured.

Some job-related criteria are naturally more objective in nature than others and can be more readily evaluated. These might include such requirements as amount and type of formal education or training, proven skills, minimum experience at a specified level of employment, acceptable appearance and verbal skills, and so forth. The candidate's ability to meet these more objective criteria can usually be evaluated quite easily through reference to well-documented and easily affirmed records, through direct questioning, or through the interviewer's direct observation of the candidate.

It is the more subjective traits—aggressiveness, drive, maturity, and so forth—that make evaluation difficult. Means of evaluating these must be carefully woven into the body of the interview to facilitate comparison of the candidate's characteristics with the job qualifications.

As we discuss ways in which various evaluative techniques can be applied, we will be thinking primarily in terms of the in-depth interview, perhaps 45 minutes to two hours in duration, for the highly qualified technical or professional applicant. The same techniques may be modified for briefer interviews, such as preliminary screening interviews or entry-level situations, where it is impractical or unnecessary to go to this depth.

MEETING THE INTERVIEWER'S OBJECTIVES

In an earlier chapter, we substantiated the need for the interviewer to determine the exact job specifications, including the desirable characteristics for the job family in question, during the preparatory stage. Prior to the interview, we said, his objectives for the interview should be well in mind, and these should be specific enough to allow the interviewer to judge how well the applicant fits the most crucial of the job specifications and to what degree he exhibits the most desirable characteristics or traits for his job family.

Assuming that this has been done and the objectives are well established, the interviewer must still find a means of getting at these objectives during the interview. In other words, he must find a way of extracting from the candidate, and then correctly interpreting, the kinds of information that will enable him to evaluate the candidate on each of several traits. The cone system outlined in the preceding chapter is perhaps the best vehicle for this sort of comprehensive evaluation, especially where highly subjective traits are involved.

Mini-Cones

In our discussion of the cone system of interviewing in Chapter 6, we mentioned the use of moderate-focus probes within the cone to reveal subjective traits and attitudes. The degree to which these are explored depends, of course, on the depth of knowledge required. In a screening interview, the occasional isolated probe, following up a candidate's statement, might be enough to establish an accurate indication of job-related attitudes. In the comprehensive evaluation interview, on the other hand, the interviewer will want to set up carefully planned mini-cones within each broad cone, with each mini-cone targeted at an important trait or attitude. Series of mini-cones not only help define objectives and ensure that they will be met; they also aid in organizing and structuring the interview in a systematic fashion.

Let's examine a specific situation to see how this might work. Steve is interviewing Beth, an electrical engineer, for a middle-management position where she would head a project group charged with the development of new, highly experimental electrical products. In planning his interview, Steve has decided to run a broad cone on Beth's involvement as founder of a college women's athletic organization and separate cones on both of her two previous jobs.

Steve has also established priorities for his interview objectives by selecting several primary job criteria (in addition to the more obvious and easily substantiated criteria such as adequate educational background) and several second-level criteria. Although Steve may have a list of 20 or more desirable traits for this job family—technological management—he knows he cannot explore each of them in great depth during an hour's time. He will listen carefully for any information that will give him insight into any of these 20 or more areas, and he may probe briefly into any or all of them in response to keys or flags offered by Beth, but his priority characteristics are the ones which he will systematically program into mini-cones.

For Beth's interview Steve has selected communication skills, drive, interpersonal relations, and planning and organizational ability as his number-one priorities for in-depth exploration. His second-level priorities are leadership, energy level, self-discipline, and maturity.

Since communication skills is a more objective characteristic, Steve will not program the investigation of this trait into a specific cone but will be on the alert throughout the interview so that he can evaluate Beth in this important area on the basis of her verbal behavior. The remaining characteristics on his priority list are more subjective in nature and will need to be carefully programmed into specific cones for investigation.

Steve has decided to nondirectively explore these characteristics as follows:

In Cone #1, he will explore Beth's outside activity (founding a college women's athletic organization), looking for evidence of her energy level, interpersonal relations, leadership, planning and organizational ability, and drive. (If there is resistance to the exploration of outside activities, he will try to explain their job-relatedness without tipping his hand.)

In Cone #2, he plans to explore her first job as electrical engineer with XYZ Electronics, looking for evidence of energy level, maturity, drive, interpersonal relations, and self-discipline.

In Cone #3, he will inquire into Beth's second and most recent job as engineering project director for J & B Systems, exploring her drive, leadership, interpersonal relations, self-discipline, and planning and organizational ability.

The broad cones and their corresponding mini-cones for Beth's interview might be diagrammed as shown in Figure 7.1. Notice that each characteristic which has been assigned a priority for investigation has been programmed into mini-cones in more than one cone. Later, we will discuss the reason for this duplication.

The mini-cones, of course, may be conducted in any order within their cone that seems most logical and natural to Steve as the interview progresses. Often, the applicant will say something, in response to the open-focus question at the top of the major cone, which provides a natural transition to one or more of the mini-cones. If not, a moderate-focus question can be utilized by the interviewer to introduce the mini-cone.

Let's listen in on portions of Steve's interview with Beth to see how he actually conducts a mini-cone. In this excerpt from their conversation, Steve has already introduced the broad cone on Beth's

Figure 7.1   Cones and Mini-Cones

Cone 1: Founding of Women's Athletic Organization

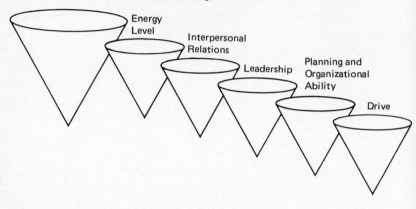

Cone 2: First Job

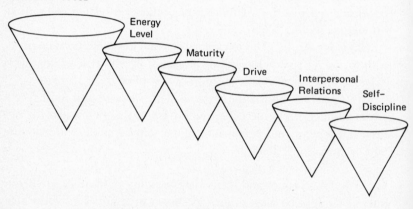

Cone 3: Most Recent Job

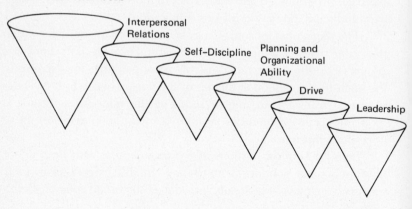

most recent job, and Beth has told him quite a bit about her duties as a leader of a technological project group there. Now Steve is ready to introduce a mini-cone to evaluate Beth's drive, that is, her ability to work without close supervision. The conversation might go as follows:

STEVE: Would you describe the kind of supervision you were given on this job?

BETH: Well, it was very loose and unstructured. We were given a long-range target, but it was left up to us how we would organize and get the job done.

STEVE: If you were to pick out the favorable points of this type of supervision, what would they be?

BETH: It made the work very exciting, because we never really knew whether we were on the right track until we put all the components together to see if it really worked. Once I came in on Friday night and discovered that a system we had developed was working. I was still there Sunday morning, just from excitement.

STEVE: Were there any less favorable aspects of being very loosely supervised?

BETH: Oh, sure. One is that we were working without any specifications; for long periods of time we didn't have any feedback as to how we were doing in management's eyes. I would have preferred a little more feedback—not just for myself but because some of the people in my group tended to want benchmarks other than those we set up for ourselves.

STEVE: If you had to select the kind of system you'd like to work in, anywhere between totally unstructured and highly structured, what would it be?

BETH: Well, I don't care to work under close supervision, but I do like to have some checkpoints, even if they are artificial—as they sometimes have to be in highly experimental work. For instance, I think that maybe every three months or six months it would be good to be able to say, "I was supposed to get this far, and I actually got beyond that, and now I know what I am supposed to accomplish in the next three months," instead of having one final goal several years away. I also like a little subtle feedback along the way. These little indications of what you are doing well and what you are doing wrong help you to learn and grow in your position. And I would like to work more closely with my supervisor in terms of where my own project fits into the scheme of things in terms of budgeting, schedules, long-term goals, and so forth.

STEVE: You tended not to see that?

BETH: No, all that was done two levels above me; it was hard to visualize how our own little project fit into the overall goals and constraints of the organization. I would have preferred to be able to understand our project in this context, so that I could have communicated it to the rest of the project group. I think this kind of knowledge would have given them extra incentive, as compared with working for years on an isolated project which they didn't really understand the importance of or the company's interest in.

Later on in this same cone exploring Beth's latest job, Steve wants to get at some more of Beth's feelings about leadership and management. Specifically, he hopes to learn whether she feels it is important for a technological manager to keep abreast of technological advances or whether she is inclined to stress her managerial skills while leaving technological know-how to those she manages. Here, Beth herself leads into the mini-cone by providing a flag, or key, that allows Steve to pursue the topic naturally.

BETH: At first, I found it difficult to try to manage and to keep up with technological advances in the field at the same time. I had worked for technical people who couldn't manage, and I was determined to concentrate on developing my management skills, but soon I found I was falling behind in the technological areas.

STEVE: Were you able to remedy this?

BETH: Yes, to a certain extent. Once I had developed my management skills and become more comfortable in a management role, I found that I could devote less time to the actual mechanics of managing and more time to keeping up with technology. But it was made difficult because I was managing people whose areas of specialization were quite different from my own major field.

STEVE: Do you feel it's necessary for a project manager to understand in depth the technology of the area that he or she is managing?

BETH: Well, I'm still wrestling with that question. A few years ago, I would have said no. I felt it was academic and if you could manage, you could manage everything. Since then I've been exposed to managers who know nothing, and that is very dangerous. I'm not sure where the dividing line is, but I know for sure I couldn't manage a professional football team because I've never played football. Now, how far away from that can you drift, I'm not sure. I do know that as a manager I don't want to be forced to make decisions on technological aspects that are totally unfamiliar to me. I think a good manager can ask her specialists for specific data on which to base her decisions if they are in technological areas where she needs help, but she has to know enough about the technology to have some framework for evaluating that data once she gets it.

STEVE: Maybe that was somewhat of an unfair question. Many management seminars have spent a lot of time and study on it, and I don't think it's been resolved yet. But I was interested in your opinion.

BETH: Well, I have to resolve it for myself if I intend to keep managing in technological areas. But I don't think you can resolve it once and for all. I think it has to be a dynamic thing. Sometimes there's a little lull in technological advances, and you can keep abreast of it while still concentrating more on the management aspects. But at other times or in other job situations, the managerial aspects of your job might prevent you from keeping up with technology as much as you would like. So it has to fluctuate a little. But I do know I wouldn't feel at ease in a strictly managerial role, with no technological knowledge or involvement at all.

Resisting the Unsupported Conclusion

Students of interviewing techniques often ask why it is necessary to run the same mini-cone in each of several broad cones. Why not run one mini-cone on drive, they ask, and then go on to some other desirable trait, thus covering several times as many traits in the course of the interview?

The answer is simple. If a mini-cone for a subjective trait or characteristic, such as drive, is run only once, the interviewer may be in danger of reaching a conclusion without adequate evidence. To resist such unsupported conclusions, we often use a device called "triangulation"—so named because our conclusion is based on a three-sided investigation rather than on one indicator. If we run the same mini-cone three times, approaching the subject in different ways each time, and get three positive indications for the characteristic under consideration, we can be three times as certain that the candidate actually exhibits that trait. Otherwise, we are unable to determine whether his or her one indication of that trait was valid or whether it was an isolated fluke which would be negated if we were to look for other indications. This is the "averaging" technique or "hedging our bets" that we mentioned early in this chapter.

Sometimes, of course, a candidate may give positive indications of a trait in two of the three mini-cones and negative indications in the other. The interviewer will then want to try to determine the reason for this apparent contradiction. For instance, a person who exhibits a negative drive on his first job but very positive drive on his two more recent jobs might be assumed to have developed more drive and self-motivation as he gained greater self-confidence and clarified his own goals. But if a person exhibited a great deal of drive and self-motivation on his first two jobs, and very little on his most recent job, the interviewer would certainly want to delve more deeply into the reasons for this loss of drive and its possible implications for the applicant's future prospects.

When flags are picked up during the course of the interview, the interviewer may also use triangulation techniques in following these up if he or she is unsure about their meaning after the first use of probes.

Unfortunately, triangulation for each priority characteristic may take too long to be feasible in the brief interview. Consequently, the interviewer may have to pursue only once those questions to which he received a seemingly definitive answer and concentrate on triangulating those characteristics which seem less clear-cut. Assume, for example, that after running the first cone in Beth's interview, Steve was convinced of her high energy level but not quite so sure about her leadership abilities. In this case, he might well abandon his plans to devote a mini-cone in the second cone to energy level, substituting leadership instead. If a choice must be made, it is best to save time to triangulate the number-one priority characteristics, if necessary, rather than to try unsuccessfully to triangulate all number-one and number-two priorities in too brief a time period.

Maintaining the Flow of Communication

In exploring these subjective traits through the use of mini-cones, it is important to keep the applicant from becoming defensive or from "clamming up." This can usually be accomplished if a friendly and permissive climate has been established at the outset of the interview and if the interviewer is careful to phrase his questions and his responses neutrally. It is most important when probing the attitudes and feelings of the applicant to avoid the implication that there is a "right" or a "wrong" answer. Instead, the interviewer should strive to give the impression that he is simply interested in the candidate's opinions. Naturally, leading questions must be scrupulously avoided.

Occasionally, after a candidate has answered difficult questions candidly, it helps to reinforce the idea that this has not been a "test" with one right answer. Notice that Steve did this in the mini-cone investigating Beth's management philosophy when he told Beth that management seminar groups had been struggling for years with the management versus technology question.

If the candidate appears to be upset by a question or reluctant to answer candidly, a little "stroking" might be necessary. Stroking is a technique whereby the interviewer soothes the candidate or calms ruffled feelings so that communication can continue. Usually a well-placed compliment or a little ego-building will do the job.

INDICATORS OF OBJECTIVE AND SUBJECTIVE TRAITS

Interviewers frequently have trouble recognizing the signs indicating that a specific personal characteristic does or does not exist in the candidate. "It is all very well to tell us to program investigation of these traits into our cones," they say, "but how do we phrase our questions to get at these traits, and how will we know we have found indications that they exist?"

Some desirable characteristics, of course, are more easily detected than others. In the case of a sales candidate, for instance, it is fairly simple to determine whether he has the education and experience called for in the job specifications. Furthermore, we can determine certain things about the quality of his performance on previous jobs: Did he achieve sales goals? How frequently? If not, why not? Is there evidence of promotions, merit raises, additional responsibilities, awards for winning sales contests, or other indications of outstanding work?

But when we get into more nebulous, increasingly subjective characteristics, many interviewers have no idea what to look for as indications of these traits. While this is, to a certain extent, a skill which the interviewer acquires through practice and experience, we have outlined some of the types of things an interviewer can be on the lookout for when seeking evidence of some of the most commonly desired traits or characteristics for new employees. (Of course, not every job will require all of these characteristics, nor have they been listed in any order of priority or importance. As we have discussed, each organization or interviewer will have to decide which characteristics are important to a specific job and then assign priorities within this list.)

Appearance. What is the overall impact of the "whole person" on the observer? Does the individual exhibit good grooming, neatness of dress, appropriateness of dress, expressiveness of features? (Caution: Minimize personal feelings and preferences and consider job needs objectively. With counseling, would the candidate consider modifications in dress or grooming to more nearly conform to organization norms?)

Personality. Does the individual give the impression of being confident but not cocky or know-it-all?

Communication Skills. Does the indvidual have the ability to listen? Are his words properly chosen? Is sentence content organized? Is his vocabulary level appropriate and grammar correct? Is he too verbose? (If written skills are important, ask for papers or articles that the candidate has previously prepared, verifying that it is his own work.)

Mechanical Aptitude. Short of giving an approved and validated mechanical aptitude test, the interviewer may pose some hypothetical mechanical problems to sample this characteristic if it is crucial.

Analytical Ability. Does the candidate demonstrate the ability to synthesize a complex set of facts and get to the point of the problem? (Guard against those who tend to either confound or oversimplify a problem.)

Numerical Ability. If this is necessary, propose some hypothetical problems to assess mathematical acumen.

Interpersonal Relations. Is the individual flexible enough to relate to differing levels or types of peers, subordinates, and/or clients? Can he or she adjust to periods of no personal contact if this is a characteristic of the position? Are there indications of changes in behavior when under extreme pressure?

Awareness. Is the individual sensitive to the situation, the environment, and the other individuals involved? Does he seem perceptive of the needs of the interviewer, or does the latter have to "draw him a picture" of what he wants from him during the interview?

Drive. Does the individual have the self-motivation to meet schedules and short-range objectives without close supervision?

Work Ethic. How well does the individual face up to his or her responsibilities?

Energy Level. Are there indicators of accomplishment in the person's background that are convincing evidence of ability to handle the physical and mental stress of the job? Is he lively (not just active) in the interview? Many high-energy people are involved in numerous outside activities, especially highly physical ones.

Aggressiveness. Is this a competitive individual who is willing to "close the sale?" Does she enjoy competition and winning? (An overly aggressive person can alienate others, so that this characteristic becomes a detriment rather than an asset. Is there evidence of this in the candidate's behavior during the interview or on previous jobs?)

Realistic Motivation. Are short-, mid-, and long-range goals in keeping with the individual's abilities? Explore for past evidence of this.

Goal vs. Task Orientation. Does the individual recognize the difference between a goal and a task that leads to the achievement of that goal? Or does he view the task as the ultimate goal? (Example: Is calling on 20 potential customers a day a goal, or is it a task that leads to the goal of meeting a sales quota?)

Self-Discipline. Is the person willing to sacrifice in order to achieve success or to reach long-range goals?

Tolerance to Failure. Is every "turndown" or failure taken personally as a severe blow to the ego? Does it interfere with the individual's ability to press on and carry out the task at hand? How has this individual adjusted to cope with a failure on a previous job or in some other undertaking?

Maturity. Can the individual learn from failure, or does he or she blame others and repeat the same mistakes? Can he use self-correction, admit errors, and recognize his own self-development needs? Does he have clear intentions and goals (not just fabricated for the interview), perspective on his own experience, and appreciation for the contributions of others?

Planning and Organizational Ability. Have the applicant take you through a typical project she has managed, from the planning and goal-setting phase to completion. Is her thinking logical, organized, and precise? Or is it fuzzy, obtuse, illogical, and vague? Can she manage time to effectively utilize the working day? Does she set priorities and put first things first?

Leadership. Are there examples of leadership in the applicant's background? Start a discussion on how she leads, disciplines, manages, handles conflict situations, and so forth. How does her philosophy and style of management blend with that of the organization?

Tact. Are there positive indicators in the interview that this individual is aware of situations and is careful in his approach to sensitive areas? Or is he clumsy and crude in his interview behavior and relations with others?

Tough-Mindedness. Does this person demonstrate mental discipline and objectivity in making decisions? Are there examples in his background where he had to make decisions that were unpopular and worked to the disadvantage of his other interests? How did he face up to these decisions? What were his feelings and thoughts about being placed in this role?

As the novice interviewer gains experience, he or she will gradually develop a feeling for the kinds of statements or behavior that indicate the presence of a particular characteristic in the applicant. They will want to keep a record of the kinds of indicators they are using for each trait, especially if several other interviewers are looking for candidates within the same job family, so that they can use the same sets of indicators to develop a greater degree of consistency in their evaluations.

CHARTING THE EVALUATION

At this point, the reader may well ask, "How can we remember and quantify all these responses?" In Chapter 2, we cautioned against note-taking in the interview. However, we will back down just a little here. If you are conducting an in-depth interview which might last from 45 minutes to an hour and a half or more and if you know from experience that your recall is less than accurate after an interview of this duration, then note-taking can be sanctioned if it is done very quickly, with the interviewer being aware of its effect on the candidate at all times. If you do take notes, remember to begin by recording a positive rather than a negative comment, and take pains to disguise the content of your notes from the candidate. Never, never rate the candidate on any sort of scale or fill out anything resembling an evaluation form in his presence, as the candidate will often become nervous or defensive if he sees that this is being done even if he can't see exactly what you are rating. Leave such forms to be completed after the candidate departs.

Once the interview has been concluded and the applicant has departed, the interviewer should record his evaluations right away while the details of the interview are fresh in his mind. Many interviewers like to use a chart such as the one shown in Figure 7.2 for rating personal characteristics.

The evaluation chart in this figure is the one Steve used in his interview with Beth. It represents the characteristics pinpointed by his organization as desirable for the engineering job family plus additional desirable characteristics for project leaders within this job family. In addition to rating Beth and the other candidates on each characteristic, based on his opinion after the interview, Steve circles or otherwise indicates those characteristics that were his top priorities

Figure 7.2   Sample Evaluation Chart for Personal Characteristics

ENGINEERING JOB FAMILY

Name of Candidate: _____

Name of Interviewer: _____

1. Educational Background	0————————4
2. Work Experience	0————————4
3. Appearance	0————————4
4. Personality	0————————4
5. Communication Skills	0————————4
6. Mechanical Ability	0————————4
7. Analytical Ability	0————————4
8. Numerical Ability	0————————4
9. Interpersonal Relations	0————————4
10. Awareness	0————————4
11. Drive	0————————4
12. Work Ethic	0————————4
13. Energy Level	0————————4
14. Self-Discipline	0————————4
15. Maturity	0————————4

(ADDITIONAL FOR PROJECT LEADERS)

16. Planning and Organizational Ability	0————————4
17. Leadership	0————————4
18. Tact	0————————4
19. Tough-Mindedness	0————————4

Additional Comments:

and his secondary priorities for investigation. He also jots down comments, where appropriate, to help him remember later why he rated each candidate as he did.

Steve then goes back to the job specification sheet for this position (see Chapter 4), indicating whether the candidate can, in his opinion, meet all the requirements and conditions of the job. These two documents, taken together, allow Steve to compare all the candidates he has interviewed for this position. Furthermore, if other interviewers are also interviewing for the same position, all of them have a common basis, in the form of these two evaluation sheets, for comparing their applicants. This sort of cross-candidate and cross-interviewer comparison can greatly enhance the validity of the selection process, and it can also be invaluable in defending the organization against possible antidiscrimination suits in which the organization is responsible for proving that a minority member was turned down for job-related reasons.

We should stress once again the need for each organization to develop its own evaluation sheets and job specification sheets, based on its own characteristics and the job families it employs. There is no all-purpose evaluation chart which can reflect the suitability of the applicant to your own organization and your particular job, no matter how carefully it is filled out. The only evaluation tools that can do this are the ones you design around your own needs and validate within your own environment.

BIASES AND PREJUDICES IN EVALUATION

In Chapter 3, we discussed some of the ways in which biases, prejudices, and ways of perceiving things can cause the interviewer to react to the applicant in certain ways that are detrimental to the communication process in the course of the interview. When it comes time to evaluate the candidate, of course, these biases and prejudices can go right on working in his or her absence unless the interviewer guards against them scrupulously. If he allows them to affect his thinking while he is evaluating or rating the candidate, the validity of the evaluation process can be seriously impaired.

During evaluation, the interviewer must examine his own biases, prejudices, and present psychological field as they relate to the candidate. How does he or she view the applicant? Does the applicant represent a class or category of people upon whom the interviewer tends to look down? Did the interviewer instinctively stereotype the candidate, or was he turned off or turned on by some irrelevant factor early in the interview? Did he applicant pose a threat to the interviewer or make him feel inferior? Did the interviewer cause the interviewing process to deteriorate and thus modify the behavior of the applicant through immature actions of his own? Is the interviewer under such pressure to fill the job that he could be seeing a very marginal candidate as a superstar based on the concept of relativity?

The interviewer should also review what he knows about the candidate's psychological field. How did he or she perceive the interview? Was it so threatening to him that it modified his behavior? How badly does he want the job? Could he be masking some of his true feelings or attitudes to mislead the interviewer? Or could he be failing to present himself in a favorable light, despite certain outstanding characteristics, because of certain factors in his background or in his present psychological make-up?

If the interviewer recognizes some of these factors that can impinge on the effectiveness of the evaluation process, he or she can make some adjustment to modify their effect and to ensure that the final evaluation represents, as nearly as is humanly possible, the "real" characteristics of the candidate rather than the characteristics falsely protrayed by a nervous or disadvantaged candidate or falsely perceived by a biased or prejudiced interviewer.

Chapter 8
Managing the Interview

Even the best-planned interviews may go astray when the interviewer loses control of the situation. The successful interviewer must learn to manage both the interview itself, in terms of his use of time and inclusion of objectives, and the candidate he is interviewing.

HOW MUCH CONTROL?

When we say that the interviewer must maintain control, we do not mean, obviously, that she should dictate every move that is made by the applicant. Most managers have a very strong tendency to overpower the applicant. This is typically true of managers who are high on the aggression scale and are accustomed to taking charge of any situation. They fail to realize that if they want to get to know the "real" candidate, they will have to set the stage to allow that person to emerge and express himself in the interview. Provision of an interview environment in which the candidate feels free to do this requires a great deal of restraint on the part of some interviewers. They must literally forbid themselves to exercise their tendencies to take over completely. Many feel that it is a sign of weakness to let the candidate feel he or she has any real input into the interview, but these interviewers will have to overcome this feeling if they are to learn anything of significance about their applicant.

On the other side of the coin is the less aggressive manager or interviewer who allows the candidate to completely assume charge of the interview. The candidate can, if she wishes, simply run right over this interviewer, leading the interview in the direction she chooses. The result is that time runs out in the interview before the interviewer has even begun to meet his objectives. Occasionally interviewers who started out as too aggressive have attempted to change and have done a complete about-face, with the result that they exercise no control at all over the interview and let the candidate run rampant.

Between these two extremes of excessive control and insufficient control, there is a very fine line representing just the right amount of control. If you have succeeded in getting the candidate to participate freely, establishing a comfortable and nonthreatening climate, and have accomplished your objectives while leaving the candidate with the feeling that she has had maximum opportunity to express herself, display her qualifications, and obtain the answers to her questions, then you have probably exercised just the right amount of control during the interview. Admittedly, this takes practice and self-evaluation, but it is well worth the effort.

MANAGING TO UTILIZE TIME EFFECTIVELY

As we have stressed in previous chapters, time during the interview must be managed effectively if the interviewer is to achieve his objectives and learn as much as possible about the candidate before he runs out of time. This is especially true in situations such as the screening interview, where brief interviews are apt to be scheduled without a break and where the interviewer is not at liberty to detain the candidate until he has explored all the topics that interest him. The cone system of interviewing lends itself exceptionally well to situations in which time must be managed tightly. It is especially useful if an assessment has to be made on a number of applicants by the end of the day.

In Chapter 6, we discussed the number of cones that could be run in a given period of time and the number of questions that were appropriate for each cone. In a 30-minute interview with a 15-minute assessment phase, we said three 5-minute cones would be about right. A 5-minute cone with normal or average communication on the applicant's part would typically contain about 8–12 questions. If the applicant is very loquacious—a real "talker"—the interviewer might ask only three or four questions during the cone. This could mean some lack of control unless the interviewee is exceptionally articulate, organized, and sensitive to the needs of the interviewer. With the bashful "nontalker," on the other hand, the tendency is for the interviewer to move toward the bottom of the cone with more direct questions. This can extend to as many as 20 or 25 questions per 5-minute cone if most of the answers border on "yes" and "no," and a very tightly controlled situation results. Later in this chapter, we will discuss some techniques that enable the interviewer to cope with these situations, in order to manage his time better.

Above all, time management in the interview does take practice. Periodically during the interview, the interviewer must ask himself: "Am I on target?" "What is happening to put me off schedule?" "How must I change my tactics or deal with this applicant to get back on target?"

The first step in effective time management, then, is awareness of the existing situation. The next step is the use of techniques to control the input and output of both participants in the interview, so that the specified objectives can be attained within the time limitations. Some interviewers intuitively develop a feeling for managing their time and their candidates during the interview. Others have to work very hard to become effective managers. Practice and experience with the interview process as a whole and with the cone system of interviewing in particular should enhance the interviewer's abilities to effectively manage time to reach his or her objectives in the interview.

MANAGING DIFFICULT APPLICANTS

The "Nontalker"

Nontalkers are usually reticent, withdrawn, anxious, frightened, or just plain reluctant or naive. Whatever the reason they are not talking, the key lies in making them comfortable in the interview situation. First, the interviewer will want to try to determine what has made the applicant uncomfortable and to remedy or avoid the offending situation.

Many applicants are turned off by preliminaries to the interview—receiving an unfriendly welcome from the secretary or receptionist, having to wait for an inordinate period of time while the "busy" manager attends to other matters, or being rapidly ushered into an unfriendly, sterile, or even hostile atmosphere.

The initial impact the interviewer has on the candidate can be critical. Does he appear arrogant, unfriendly, cold, or aloof, or is he "gushing" and just plain phony? Does he seem to be genuinely pleased to see the candidate and interested in talking with him, or is this just another unpleasant task which he wishes to put behind him as quickly as possible?

Often, the interviewer can turn the potential nontalker into a cooperative participant during the first minute or two of the interview. He should bring him into a controlled and friendly setting, where they will be private and uninterrupted. He should begin with a friendly discussion while the candidate adjusts to the surroundings and the interviewer. He should do some structuring to let the applicant know how the interview is going to proceed and then start with an open-focus question (but not *too* open) in a topic area that is not threatening to the applicant.

Some other techniques that work well with nontalkers are:

Try to keep the candidate up toward the middle or top of the cone with moderate-focus questions.

Begin with a topic that is positive to the candidate to build his confidence, and do some positive stroking to encourage him.

Don't worry about getting into the main objectives of the interview until you have made the applicant comfortable and have helped him to feel a part of the communication process. Building solid lines of communication must become your number-one objective when dealing with the nontalker.

Handle any sensitive areas with extreme care.

Be aware of the applicant's feelings. This is essential to effecting successful communication with a reticent respondent.

A typical nonproductive attitude on the part of the interviewer is the assertion that the nontalker must "sell himself." "If he can't sell me, I don't want him," some interviewers say. "It's his job to establish a line of communication, not mine." This attitude has led to the loss of many potentially fine employees. Many times when the initial reticence of an applicant is overcome with a little help from the interviewer, the latter is pleasantly surprised at the quality of the person who is allowed to emerge.

The "Talker"

The overly aggressive, verbose, even "windy" applicant, if allowed to go unchecked, can be very detrimental to the interviewer's efforts to achieve interview objectives. Some techniques which might prove useful in controlling the talker are:

> Carefully interrupt, excusing yourself if necessary, when the talker pauses for a breath. Try to pose a question which relates in some way to the topic of the talker's choice but which will allow you to fulfill one or more of your own objectives.

> If this is not possible, interrupt to get the candidate's attention and then restructure as follows: "John, I'm very interested in all your outside activities. However, in the interest of time, could we move on to talk about your last job?"

> Keep the talker in or near the bottom of the cone with more moderate and direct questions. This tactic gives him less chance to wander far afield from the topic you have selected.

> Continue using polite interruptions and restructuring to keep the applicant on track if this continues to be necessary. All but the most obtuse will eventually get the idea that the interviewer intends to select the topics of conversation to suit his or her interview plan.

This is one situation in which the interviewer simply cannot afford to be shy or overly polite. If he fails to take charge of the interview and gives the candidate so little direction that the latter dictates the direction of the interview, the candidate, if she is verbal at all, will roam from topic to topic at will. Whether she is a natural-born talker or is talking excessively from nervousness or from a desire to avoid certain topics by pursuing others, she can soon undermine the interview if not taken in tow. Some sophisticated applicants, sensing an insecure interviewer who is afraid to control the situation, may even reverse the questioning procedure, ending up by interrogating the interviewer. The overly permissive interviewer who allows this to happen is liable to end up without any useful information about the candidate, and much of the time he will also fail to earn the candidate's respect.

In handling the talker, it is very important to maintain that fine line of just the right amount of control. The interviewer should not try to squelch the applicant to the point where the latter is offended. Judgment is very important in determining just how much control to impose on the talker.

The Coached Applicant

The coached applicant is most often found on college campuses or among recent college graduates, but any candidate may have had instruction in how to behave and respond during the interview. Often this applicant has had a seminar or has read literature on how to prepare for the interview. He may be carefully schooled on what to do and what not to do to present the proper image to the interviewer, or he may have become exceedingly polished in his presentation as a result of exposure to 10 or 15 company recruiters.

The danger is that the interviewer can be badly misled by the coached applicant. Many are so skilled in presenting what they think the interviewer or the organization wants to see that they do not present themselves as they really are.

Early in the interview, or even prior to its beginning, the interviewer should try to determine whether he or she is likely to be dealing with a coached applicant. If the interview is taking place on a campus where a seminar in interviewing is offered by the placement office or if the student volunteers the information that he has participated in a great many interviews, then chances are good that he has been coached. If so, the interviewer's task is to effectively penetrate the facade or cover that the applicant has been taught to adopt and get to the "real" applicant.

Since the coached applicant often is taught how to answer certain questions properly, the interviewer should try to avoid these questions or at least to be alert for answers that sound too rehearsed or phony. Figure 8.1 lists some of the questions on which students are commonly coached. Many of these questions have some solid objectives behind them (although others do not) but are much overused, and most applicants are conditioned to the proper, "impressive" responses. To avoid getting these "canned" responses and to increase the chance that you will get to know the real applicant, use the cone system, working your objectives into the cone nondirectively by pursuing flags that the applicant supplies while answering open-focus and moderate-focus questions.

If you really need to ask some of these cliché questions, be sure to pursue them down to the second and third level of depth. Probe deeply into the answer to see if the response was really one of substance or just a practiced superficial answer intended to satisfy or impress the interviewer.

Interviewers who have had some experience with this type of applicant soon learn to recognize the quickly given and glib practiced response which is often characterized by its inappropriate shallowness in comparison with the depth of the interviewer's question. The best defense is the skillful use of the cone system, so that the coached

Figure 8.1   Some Questions Frequently Rehearsed by Coached Candidates

1. What are your vocational goals for the future?
2. What type of position are you interested in at the present time? Why?
3. What qualifications do you have that suit you for this line of work?
4. What personal characteristics are necessary to succeed in your field?
5. What position in our organization would you choose if you were able to pick freely?
6. What are the disadvantages of the field you have chosen?
7. Do you like routine work? Regular or irregular hours?
8. What do you know about our organization?
9. Why do you think you want to work for us?
10. What determines a person's progress in a large corporation?
11. Would you rather work for a small company or a large one? Why?
12. Tell me how you think modern industry is operated.
13. Why are you interested in our company's products?
14. How much money do you hope to make at the beginning? How much at age 30? At age 40?
15. What type of environment do you prefer to live in?
16. Do you prefer a specific geographic location? Why?
17. Would you be willing to go wherever the company assigns you?
18. What is the most important thing you have learned from the previous jobs you have held?
19. Are you more interested in making money or in serving your fellows?
20. Would you rather work by yourself or with others?
21. What sort of boss would you choose to work for?
22. What have you done that shows willingness to work (creativeness, initiative, etc.)?
23. Are you willing to fight to get ahead?
24. What characteristics do you look for in your best friends?
25. Are you greatly concerned with pleasing other people?
26. What is your major strength? What is your major weakness?
27. Do you like to receive a lot of attention?
28. Define cooperation (success, etc.).

Figure 8.1   (*Continued*)

---

29. What types of people seem to "rub you the wrong way?"
30. Do you have trouble being tolerant of persons who are appreciably different from you?
31. Which of your parents has had the greatest influence on you? In what way?
32. Tell me about your home life during the time you were growing up.
33. How do you get along with your family now?
34. At what age did you first contribute to the family income?
35. How do you usually spend your weekends?
36. How did you spend your vacations while you were in school?
37. What kinds of books and magazines do you usually read?
38. How often do you entertain at home or in your apartment?
39. How often do you go out? Where do you go, and what do you like to do?
40. Do you think potential employers should consider a student's grades? Why?
41. How did you happen to go to college?
42. Why did you select this particular major?
43. Why did you select this particular school?
44. If you were starting again as a freshman, what major and what courses would you select? Why?
45. Do you think you have done the best scholastic work of which you are capable?
46. Were your extracurricular activities worth the time you spent on them? Why or why not?
47. Would you be willing to forget all about your education and start over again from scratch?
48. Tell me a story!

---

candidate is faced with moderate-focus questions to which there are no canned answers.

The Practiced Applicant

Unlike the coached applicant, the practiced applicant is usually very smooth and professional as a result of having been in the job market on more than one occasion. Many practiced applicants are persons who frequently "shop" for jobs, even though they are employed, just to keep a fix on their value in the employment marketplace. The practiced applicant can be very interview-wise, since he has been exposed to all the gimmicks in the interviewer's repertoire. For the same reason, he can easily be turned off, or he can turn the interview into an exercise in gamesmanship.

The interviewer who is faced with a practiced applicant must be friendly, mature, businesslike, and professional in conducting the interview. He should lay out the interview structure, explaining exactly what he would like to accomplish. If the interviewer acts as if he knows what he is doing while giving the applicant every opportunity to present his credentials and if he makes an effort to meet the applicant's needs as well as his own, he will stand a good chance of being accepted readily and openly by the practiced applicant. After all, the practiced applicant has presumably had enough experience to recognize an effective interviewer when he sees one.

The "Professional" Applicant

The professional applicant is often a practiced applicant, but he has some additional credentials and peculiarities. He is usually urbane, sophisticated, and well traveled. He has probably held a high-level position in a large and prestigious organization, and he may hold advanced graduate degrees from the finest institutions in North America or Europe. Even more significant is the more than casual exposure of the professional applicant to the behavioral sciences and his sophisticated knowledge of interpersonal communications and interviewing techniques. Added to this, quite frequently, are above-average intelligence and impeccable verbal skills.

With this kind of profile, the professional applicant can be more than a handful for the nonprofessional interviewer. Thorough preparation and more than casual knowledge of interviewing techniques are essential in handling and assessing this type of candidate.

Most large organizations have executive recruiters who screen this type of candidate. These specialists have the experience, maturity, and professional interviewing training to communicate comfortably with the professional candidate. They are also trained in the assessment of this type of individual and are able to assist the executive group in hiring candidates at this level.

If your organization does not have executive recruiters, you may want to consider calling upon one of the many professional consultants who deal exclusively in the recruitment and assessment of this level of candidate. Unless you are an exceedingly experienced and accomplished interviewer, the engagement of a reputable consulting firm will save you time, money, and, possibly, disappointing results.

MEETING APPLICANT OBJECTIVES

The final portions of the interview are devoted to meeting the needs of the candidate. This, too, is an important part of interview management, since the interviewer must accomplish this goal if he or she is to leave the applicant with a good feeling about the interview and the organization.

Remember, the applicant has an important career decision to make. She will surely be eager to know certain things about the job, the organization, and the people she will work with if she gets the job. She will also want to know when she can expect to hear from you or from someone else in the organization with a job offer or a rejection. Now that the interviewer has obtained the answers to his questions, it is time to provide the information that the candidate wants. In too many interviews, this phase is completely neglected or is handled in an incomplete or ineffective manner. The result is that the candidate leaves with a feeling of dissatisfaction. She is "left hanging" and has little basis for deciding whether she wants the job even if it is offered to her.

The Influence and Sell

During the influence and sell portion of the interview, the interviewer has his chance to sell the applicant on the idea of coming to work for his organization. By saving this phase until after the assessment portion of the interview, the interviewer has gained an important advantage. Like any astute salesperson, he can first assess his "customer" and then sell to suit his needs. This is especially important in tight labor markets, where many companies may be competing for the best candidates. The interviewer may have a hard time convincing these applicants that his is the organization they should consider above all others.

In order to sell the job to the applicant, the interviewer must note, throughout the interview, the applicant's likes and dislikes, so that certain strong points of the job, from the applicant's point of view, can be incorporated into the sell. This doesn't mean, of course, that you should be dishonest. But you can capitalize on the positive aspects your company offers without misleading the applicant. Let's look at a couple of examples.

Chuck Peters, the research director of a paper manufacturing firm, was interviewing a chemical engineer. In exploring the engineer's background, Chuck learned that he had moved six times during the last four years on his previous job. His wife and family had had enough moving for a lifetime. Chuck offered the applicant a position on his company's research and development staff with the assurance that he would be in the same location for at least four years and probably more. Although the engineer had a better salary offer from an aerospace company, he took Chuck's job because it promised better stability of residence for his family. If Chuck had not been alert, he could have missed this small point in the evaluation process and lost the candidate.

On the other hand, in an interview between a woman accounting graduate who had secretarial experience and the representative of a major manufacturer, the following sequence of events unfolded. Throughout the 30-minute campus screening interview, the interviewer kept coming back to the young woman's secretarial experience. The applicant, while trying to be polite, indicated several times that she was not interested in secretarial employment. She continually emphasized her major field of study, accounting, and her 3.5 grade average. The interviewer concluded the session by trying to sell the applicant an executive secretarial position. When the company offered her a location visit, she naturally turned it down. Soon after, she accepted an accounting position with a chemical firm. The interviewer had lost a candidate he considered outstanding because he completely misread or ignored the clues and sold the wrong position.

Now, let's return for a moment to Sam, the young man we discussed in Chapter 5. As you remember, Sam had conflicting goals. He was torn between a pharmaceutical sales job, which would enable him to support his wife but would require him to quit graduate school in social work; a service station job, which would allow him to continue school and still contribute a little to the family income; or continuing in graduate school while his wife continued to support him.

Let's assume that Brad, the interviewer, is very impressed with Sam and believes his company would benefit from having him as an employee. If Brad had not bothered to find out the total picture of Sam's psychological field and the various goals that were causing indecision on his part, he may well have tried to sell a sales position on the basis of its high pay, its good incentive program, the interesting travel involved, the joys of intense competition with other salesmen, and the social aspects of the job, such as attending cocktail parties and taking clients out to dinner. Sam is interested in making money, but he is also interested in spending time with his wife. He wants to keep his college circle of friends, and he shies away from the business world "rat race." Chances are good that Sam will decide, on the basis of what Brad has told him, that the extra income is not worth the other sacrifices.

On the other hand, let's assume that Brad has listened attentively and has taken the trouble to understand Sam's goals. He will want to stress the salary and incentives of the job, but he will certainly want to deemphasize the excessive travel involved, and he will want to omit mention, unless specifically asked, of aspects of the job that have a high-pressure or competitive overtone. Of course, Brad will be honest about these aspects of the job if they are to be an integral part of Sam's duties, and he will answer Sam's questions directly, but he will not use these as selling points. Instead, he may stress the fact that Sam can work from his home when not traveling, thereby spending more time with his wife when he is in town.

Then, as a clincher, Brad might point out to Sam that a good pharmaceutical salesman performs a service to others by seeing that physicians and pharmacists are well informed on pharmaceutical products and options, thereby indirectly improving the health care that is available to all who deal with the salesman's clients. At this point, Sam will have something new to think about. Prior to the interview, he believed that one of his goals—preparing for a career of service to others—would have to be sacrificed if he quits graduate school in order to become a pharmaceutical salesman. By showing Sam how the sales job could fulfill this goal, Brad has made this alternative more attractive, since it will fulfill more goals than Sam originally believed it would.

Now, if Brad is interviewing for a variety of positions within his pharmaceutical firm rather than just the sales job, he can go even further. He might, for instance, offer Brad a part-time job in the customer relations department, answering questions from users of the company's products. This job, at a considerably higher salary than the part-time service station job Sam was considering, would still permit Sam to continue graduate school and would fulfill most of his other goals as well.

However you decide to sell your organization and the specific position that is available, be sincere and direct. Be meticulous in telling the truth. Don't oversell the job or make untrue promises in your efforts to make the job match the goals of the candidate, as this could lead to later disenchantment and subsequent high turnover. The interviewer who speaks with honest enthusiasm about his company is convincing. Give the applicant a brief outline of the duties of the job, the salary, and the benefits, and answer directly his questions about what he will be doing, the people he will be working with, and what the future could hold. The more specific you can be, without making false promises, the better chance you have of influencing the candidate you want. Try not to be pushy. Salaried applicants usually react more favorably to the "soft-sell" or subtle approach than to "hard-sell" approaches.

One word of caution: Don't sell a candidate a job if you are not interested in hiring her. It will not serve any purpose from your point of view as an interviewer, and it is cruel to the applicant to make her desire a position she has no hope of getting. If this is the case, just describe the job in a very general sense and react to the candidate's questions without offering any false encouragement. It is not necessary to come right out and tell the candidate that she does not qualify, but avoid projecting the candidate into the job. For example, refrain from saying "When you join our company . . ." or "You will like the people in that department." If the candidate says that she has other job offers and must make up her mind within a week, suggest that she should not wait on your company's offer, since a decision will not be made that soon. This prevents the applicant's turning down an offer in the false hope that yours may be forthcoming.

If you are unsure whether you might be interested in an applicant or not, it is better to be neutral than to get her hopes up falsely. Describe the job, the organization, and the benefits factually but briefly. Answer her questions, but don't go overboard trying to convince her that this is the job for her. If, after seeing other applicants, you decide that she was the best one after all, you can always call her back and sell her at that time.

Summary and Close

In any case, you should let the applicant know when he or she can expect to hear from you or from someone else in the company regarding your decision. This takes place during the last minute or two of the interview, during the summary phase, along with a general wind-up of the interview. During the summary, you will want to leave the applicant with the feelings that the interviewing process has been brought to a logical and successful close; a good relationship and a measure of understanding have been reached between the two participants; and the applicant knows what to expect as the next step in the process.

The interviewer might say something like: "Well, Mary, I think I've learned a lot about your skills and about what you want out of your career. I hope I've also answered most of your questions about the ABC Company, and I think you'll find, when you think it over, that our organization has a lot to offer an experienced salesperson like you. I think our incentive plan is especially tailored for a person with your drive and ambition. I'll be making my recommendations to my manager tomorrow, and I'm sure you'll be hearing from him by Monday." Then he and Mary would exchange good-byes, shake hands, and the interview would come to a close.

Here again, avoid suggesting to the unqualified or undesirable applicant that the hiring decision could be an affirmative one. Do not let the undesirable candidate pin you down on the spot as to what the final decision might be or why he may or may not meet your qualifications. Recent case decisions on discrimination have made this an extremely sensitive point in the interviewing process.

HANDLING COUNSELING SITUATIONS IN THE INTERVIEW

A great many situations arise during the course of employment interviewing which tempt the interviewer to turn into a counselor or dispenser of advice. Occasionally an interviewer will perceive that a candidate is actually confused. Perhaps he needs help in identifying his qualifications and ways in which he could more effectively present himself in the marketplace, or perhaps he needs guidance in selecting the type of career that would best utilize his skills and appeal to his interests. At other times, interviewers succumb to the temptation to go too far in explaining to a candidate the reasons that he was turned down for the job or the factors that kept him from meeting specifications. And once in a while, interviewers simply get an urge to feel important by trying to tell others how to run their lives.

All these situations present serious pitfalls to the interviewer who naively tries to step into the counseling role. In the first place, counseling in the pure sense is a strictly professional occupation and should be engaged in only by those who have sufficient training and experience to know what they are and are not qualified to attempt. In addition, regulations enforced by the Equal Employment Opportunity Commission have made certain counseling situations suspect. An interviewer who assumes an active counseling role with a rejected or about-to-be-rejected candidate can be inadvertently setting the stage for a discrimination suit against his or her organization.

Even if the advice given to the applicant is harmless and if there is no danger of a discrimination suit, the interviewer is not accomplishing his interview objectives while he is using the time for counseling. If an applicant genuinely needs counseling, the interviewer should refer him or her to one of the many state and federal agencies which are staffed to offer this sort of professional assistance (or, in the case of a campus candidate, to the counseling staff in the placement office).

A few large private companies do have the time and resources and consider it their social obligation to provide employment counseling to applicants who desire it. Obviously the interviewer who works for this type of organization and who has been assigned the responsibility of rendering this service to applicants should carry out this function—hopefully with the proper training and experience. But for the vast majority of interviewers, counseling within the selection interview setting is to be avoided at all costs. Besides wasting your valuable interview time, you may actually harm the applicant or the reputation of your organization by giving in to the temptation to give personal advice.

Chapter 9
The Law
and the Interview

In recent years, several very large industrial organizations have been so inundated with discrimination suits brought about by their use of selection techniques that they have turned the selection mechanism over to their legal departments for close scrutiny and a new set of guidelines.

Because most legal consultants are not versed in the art of interviewing, the result of this effort has been the issue of a limited list of questions to be asked of all candidates and especially entry-level candidates by the employment interviewer. The end result, of course, is a rigidly controlled patterned interview. Although this type of in-house control over the interview helps to keep the organization out of trouble with the Equal Employment Opportunity Commission (EEOC), it is rendering ineffectual the entire concept of the employment interview.

We see the pendulum swinging full course, from a completely unbridled interview, where the candidate is fair game and anything goes, to a "name, rank, and serial number" approach. The interviewer's feeling in the latter type of interview is often summarized as follows: "If they're warm, hire 'em, because if we don't and they're a minority, we've just brought another discrimination suit on ourselves." Understandably, such suits mean problems for corporations. They bring unwanted, and often unfair, negative publicity, create more work for the corporate lawyers and personnel specialists who must defend the organization before a court or a commission, and engender ill will among both those minority group members who already work for the company and those who would like to but do not.

These types of patterned interviewing policies combined with the rapid disappearance of validated testing instruments for employee selection and the increasing tendencies of organizations to refuse to release derrogatory information on previous employees have led many employers to believe they are once again relegated to coin flipping in the selection process. However, close scrutiny of the law coupled with many in-depth discussions of the subject has led most interviewing experts to believe that a middle-of-the-road position is possible. This position maintains that a skilled interviewer can still preserve the effectiveness of the interview process while complying with the law. As we will discuss in the following pages, it does place a primary obligation on interviewers to be sure they understand the framework of the law and conduct their interviews accordingly, and it requires that the organization provide interviewers with the training that will enable them to meet this obligation.

THE EFFECT OF LEGAL RESTRICTIONS

Many interviewers feel they are unable to obtain the information they need during an interview because of constraints imposed upon the interviewing process by the EEOC and by Title VII legislation. It is not necessarily true that these rules and regulations prevent interviewers from finding out what they need to know. However, it is undeniable that EEOC and Title VII regulations have radically changed the complexion of interviewing in recent years.

Some companies have taken an extreme position: Why bother even having an interview with a minority person, since there is nothing you can legally ask anyway? This is a common feeling among those who have not studied the letter and intent of the law. Although the law does put constraints on the kinds of questions that tend to discriminate against minorities, it still permits the employer to make the decision to hire the most qualified candidate, *providing* the judgment is made objectively and without prejudice and *providing* the organization does not have a pattern of discriminatory hiring decisions that screen out an entire *class* of people.

EEOC and Title VII regulations, along with recent court decisions regarding their application and interpretation, have changed the interview in a number of ways:

Increasing emphasis has had to be placed on the interviewer's development of the kind of relationship with the candidate that takes the threat out of the process. While this is just good sense any time communication needs to be established, it is especially important when a minority candidate is being interviewed, so that he or she has no reason to feel threatened or defensive to the point of striking back by filing a discrimination suit.

It has become imperative for the interviewer to assess and understand any degree of aggressiveness, hostility, or reluctance to establish two-way communication on the part of the candidate.

It has become mandatory that the interviewing process be focused on job-related topics and that the areas to be evaluated have been spelled out before the interview in the form of job specifications and essential characteristics.

The interviewer must have a thorough knowledge not only of the illegal and borderline sensitive areas peculiar to the class of candidate being interviewed, but also of the kinds of inquiries that can legally be made to enhance the assessment of this class of interviewee.

All the above seems to be a big order for a manager who must make a hiring decision, especially if he or she only employs the interviewing process on occasion. It *is* a big order, but fortunately antidiscrimination legislation has had a positive side-effect because of the magnitude of this challenge: It has given employers the impetus to provide their interviewers with professional training, so they know how to operate within the intent of the law. One result of such training is that the interviewer learns how to avoid discrimination suits. But perhaps of longer-lasting impact, he also learns to understand interviewing concepts and their application within potentially sensitive areas. He becomes a better all-around interviewer, and he is more likely to select the best-qualified candidate for the position, because he has avoided screening out certain well-qualified applicants on the basis of prejudicial judgments.

Every interviewer, whether a professional full-time interviewer or a manager who conducts an occasional screening interview, owes it to himself and his company to become familiar with the laws governing discrimination in interviewing and to comply with them. In the following section, we will discuss some of the most common federal restrictions on interviewing practices.

RESTRICTIONS IN THE INTERVIEW

A great many interviewers panic when faced by a minority candidate because they believe there is no question they can pose which will be above suspicion. In desperation, they frequently turn to the application blank provided by their organization, selecting questions from it in the belief that anything on the application must be legal under EEOC and Title VII regulations. Unfortunately, this is not necessarily a safe assumption. Many organizations, even very large and sophisticated ones, have not recently had their applications checked for legality and hence are inadvertently asking illegal questions. The EEOC has ruled that illegal application blanks, like illegal questions in the interview, can be grounds for discrimination charges, but so far most suits have been filed as a result of alleged face-to-face discrimination; thus organizations are more lax about their application blanks than they should be.

What, then, can an interviewer do to be sure he is not operating illegally within the interview? In general, he must be aware of the critical areas of concern under Title VII—that is, the classes of people against whom he may not discriminate—and the questions that he may not legitimately ask of each class. The thoughtful reader will no doubt determine, upon a review of these questions, that they are not questions that are directly related to job specifications in any case, and thus their omission does not really hamper the experienced interviewer from determining whether the applicant meets the job requirements. On the contrary, their omission from the interview simply keeps the interviewer from eliminating a candidate for reasons which are prejudicial rather than directly job-related, and that is exactly why the EEOC wants them omitted.

The major areas of EEOC's concern are outlined below, along with questions that are illegal and should be avoided by every interviewer and alternate questions that are within the law.

Discrimination on the Basis of Sex

It is very difficult for some interviewers to understand why they can't ask questions of a woman to determine how many children she has, whether she is married, how old her children are, what provisions she has made for their care, whether she is pregnant or planning to be pregnant soon, and so forth. They have been asking these questions for 30 years or more in selecting women, they say, and now all of a sudden these questions are illegal. But they need to know these answers in order to determine whether the woman should be hired or whether she will perform adequately on the job. Why can't they ask them anymore?

The law is clear. It is designed to remove the factors that enable an employer to discriminate against a minority—in this case, women. But the employer is not finished with his argument. "But I am not going to use that information to discriminate against that person," he screams. And the logical rebuttal is: "Then why do you have to ask the questions, if you aren't going to use the information?"

Some of the common questions asked by interviewers that tend to discriminate against women and should be avoided scrupulously are shown in Figure 9.1, along with alternatives that are legal. (Other illegal questions and some alternatives are shown in Figures 9.2 and 9.3.)

"But I want to hire a salesperson who will travel extensively!" wails the typical interviewer. "If I can't find out whether she has a bunch of sick kids and an unreliable babysitter and a jealous husband, how will I know if she is going to be able to meet her commitments?" The answer is simple. Think of her as a *person*, not a wife and mother, and phrase the question as you would for any other person. (You would probably not dream of asking a male applicant about the reliability of his babysitter or whether he plans to have any more children.) Explain the needs of the job and phrase the question as follows: "This position requires travel over a 400-mile territory throughout the state. This often necessitates a ten- or eleven-hour day and about two nights a week spent out in the territory. Is there any reason you might not be able to meet these commitments in the foreseeable future?" The question, phrased this way, does not violate any legal constraint, and the applicant is just as likely to answer truthfully as she would be to, say, a direct question about her childcare arrangements.

Many women who know their rights under the law might volunteer additional, very specific information if they want the position in question. An applicant might say, for instance: "I am divorced. I have three young children under the age of five, but my mother, who lives with us, is my babysitter; so there are no problems whatsoever associated with my traveling."

To be on the safe side, it is recommended that the interviewer

Figure 9.1 Legal Alternatives to Inquiries that Discriminate on the Basis of Sex

It Is ILLEGAL to Ask:	*It Is LEGAL to Ask:*
Questions concerning the original name of an applicant whose name has been changed by court order or otherwise (except as indicated in next column).	Whether the applicant has worked for your company under another name. Generally, it is not legal to ask the maiden name of a married applicant. However, those whose job it is to check with former employers may ask whether her work with them was performed under a different name.
Whether applicants are married, single, divorced, widowed, etc. Avoid invalid stereotypes and value judgments that, for instance, a divorced woman might not be as stable as a married one.	
Questions about the future marital plans of applicants.	
Questions concerning pregnancy.	
Questions concerning arrangements for child care.	
Whether an applicant's spouse objects to the applicant's travel or hours.	Whether the applicant can meet specific work schedules and whether he or she has any activities, commitments, or responsibilities that could prevent regular attendance at work.
Whether the applicant plans to start a family.	
Questions concerning the applicant's status as head of household or principal wage-earner.	
How long an applicant plans to work.	What the applicant's long-range career goals are.
Questions about a female's stand on women's liberation issues.	

respond as follows: "Thank you for volunteering that information. However, since our organization is an equal opportunity employer and we are interested only in job-related factors, what you have told me will have no bearing on whether or not you are recommended for the position, except for the fact that you are free to meet the job requirements for travel." If, in fact, you are an equal opportunity employer and have the statistics to prove it, then you are on the record as such just in case this candidate is trying to set you up for a discrimination suit by "volunteering" illegal information. Obviously, the above statement or any similar disclaimer should be made in a pleasant and matter-of-fact manner, so that the applicant will not perceive it as a threat or a put-down of any sort.

Although most concern so far has centered on discrimination against women, it should also be pointed out that males are similarly protected against sex discrimination. A man who applies for a traditionally female position, such as stenographer or nurse, is entitled to a fair chance for that position under the law, just as surely as is a woman who applies for a traditionally male position.

Discrimination on the Basis of Race, Color, or National Origin

A large portion of the discrimination suits that are filed involve alleged discrimination against persons of a minority race or color or of an alien nationality. Applicants tend to be especially sensitive and suspicious of discrimination if they are clearly, visibly different from the interviewer in terms of color or nationality or if they are members of a race that has traditionally been the object of prejudice in the past.

Of course, the interviewer cannot help noticing that these applicants appear to belong to a minority race, but he or she can certainly refrain from remarking on this fact, treating the applicant differently from nonminority candidates, or asking questions that would tend to single out the minority candidate's differences.

In addition to the obvious types of discriminatory questions, there are several areas of inquiry that would not appear to discriminate against minorities but that in fact have been judged to be discriminatory. These include questions about the economic status or credit rating of the candidate and inquiries about his or her arrest record. It has been shown that minorities as a class tend to have lower credit ratings, lower socioeconomic standing, and more frequent arrest records than nonminorities—often because they have been the victims of prejudice or discrimination in previous situations. As a result, the EEOC has concluded that to use these criteria as a basis for rejection of a candidate is to compound the effect of discrimination, and these questions have been ruled illegal.

Since many border states are in the process of passing legislation which holds an employer liable for the employment of illegal aliens, employers in these states are in a difficult position. On the one hand, they may be in trouble for hiring an alien; on the other, they may be in trouble for attempting to determine whether the candidate is an alien or not. However, EEOC regulations do permit interviewers to

Figure 9.2   Legal Alternatives to Inquiries that Discriminate on the Basis of Race, Color, or National Origin

---

It Is ILLEGAL to Ask:

Questions about the applicant's membership in clubs, fraternities, lodges, etc., *unless* you tell the applicant to omit mention of those organizations which indicate religious affiliations, national origin, race, ancestry, or color.

That an applicant submit a photograph of himself or herself *prior* to being employed.

Questions about a black applicant's stand on civil rights issues.

Questions concerning the arrest record of the applicant, because in many areas minorities are frequently arrested in situations in which nonminorities would not be arrested.

Questions about an applicant's credit rating. Indicators of economic status have a forseeably disproportionate impact on blacks as a class (charge accounts, bank accounts, type of housing, car ownership, living with relatives, bankruptcy history, garnishments, etc.). If employment is denied based on these indicators, discrimination can be charged.

Questions about the birthplace of the applicant or his or her relatives.

Whether the applicant or his relatives are citizens.

It Is LEGAL to Ask:

Questions concerning convictions, *if* you find out when, why, where, and how it came about. However, this inquiry is suspect, because more minorities tend to have been convicted, and the use made of the information is important. In some states it is unlawful to consider convictions made more than ten years ago. In Washington, you cannot inquire beyond seven years. EEOC approves a five-year cutoff.

The applicant's present residence and length of time he or she has resided in the city or state.

"If you are not a U.S. citizen, do you have a legal right to work in the U.S. and to remain here permanently?"

Figure 9.2   *(Continued)*

Questions about the applicant's national origin or ancestry, length of residency in the U.S., or commonly used language.	What languages are read, spoken, or written fluently by the applicant *if* job duties require these skills.
How the applicant learned to read, write, or speak a foreign language.	
Names and addresses of applicant's relatives. Legitimate need for this information arises only *after* the applicant is hired.	The name and address of a person to be notified in case of accident or emergency. This is legal because the inquiry is not limited to relatives, but it is still not needed until after employment.
Questions concerning the original name of an applicant whose name has been changed by court order or otherwise (except as indicated in next column).	Whether the applicant has worked for your company under another name. Generally, it is not legal to ask the maiden name of a married female applicant. However, those whose job it is to check with former employers may ask whether her work with them was performed under a different name.

ask whether the applicant has a legal right to work in the United States. If you are working in a state where the employment of illegal aliens is a widespread problem, your organization's legal counsel or employment division will no doubt develop a policy to protect your organization.

Figure 9.2 shows a number of questions that have been determined to be discriminatory against applicants of minority race, color, or national origin. Legal alternatives are also indicated.

Discrimination on the Basis of Age, Religion, and Miscellaneous Categories

At one time, may job candidates were systematically turned down if they were 40 years of age or older simply because organizations preferred to hire younger persons. Under current laws and restrictions, this practice is no longer allowed. A candidate must be turned down on the basis of job-related reasons or lack of qualifications rather than age alone. It is currently against the law to ask a candidate

Figure 9.3   Legal Alternatives to Inquiries that Discriminate on the Basis of Age, Religion, and Other Miscellaneous Categories

It Is ILLEGAL to Ask:	*It Is LEGAL to Ask:*
The age of an applicant.	Whether the applicant is over 21 (or the legal age for adulthood in your state). The number of years that an applicant worked at a previous job.
How long an applicant plans to work.	The long-range career goals of the applicant.
Questions concerning an applicant's religious denomination or affiliation. Questions such as "What holidays do you observe?" or "Who is your pastor?" are unlawful.	
Questions about the applicant's membership in clubs, fraternities, lodges, etc., *unless* you tell the applicant to omit mention of those organizations which indicate religious affiliation, national origin, race, ancestry, or color.	
Questions about an applicant's credit rating or other indicators of economic status.	
Questions concerning the arrest record of the applicant.	Questions concerning convictions, *if* you find out when, why, where, and how it came about. However, this inquiry is suspect, and the use made of the information is important. In some states it is unlawful to consider convictions made more than ten years ago. In Washington, you cannot inquire beyond seven years. EEOC approves a five-year cutoff.
Questions concerning the type of discharge the applicant received from the military.	Questions concerning the applicant's military experience in the U.S. armed forces.
	Questions about an applicant's educational background.
	Questions about the applicant's work experience.
	Questions concerning the applicant's referral to your company.

Figure 9.3   *(Continued)*

Whether the applicant can meet specific work schedules and whether he or she has any activities, commitments, or responsibilities that could prevent attending work regularly.

Questions concerning a physical or mental handicap *if* it relates to the performance of a particular job. Questions concerning any health problems which may affect work performance are also permitted.

It is also illegal to tell the applicant: "This is a Protestant (Jewish, Catholic) organization."

---

his age, although a candidate may be asked if he is 21 (or the legal age of adulthood in your state). Some states have passed legislation making it illegal to ask the candidate's birthdate or date of graduation.

Religion is another area in which discrimination is not allowed. Any questions aimed toward determining the religious affiliation of the candidate may be grounds for a discrimination suit.

Many other classes of persons may be judged to be the object of discrimination in employment. The handicapped and homosexuals are among minority groups that have the protection of antidiscrimination legislation. Because the specific rules regulating interviews with these persons, as well as the interpretation of these rules, are constantly changing, the interviewer should make himself aware of current regulations and interpretations, both at the federal level and in his own state.

Figure 9.3 contains questions that discriminate by age, religion, and miscellaneous categories, with legal alternatives.

OTHER PREEMPLOYMENT RESTRICTIONS

There are many other practices and procedures relating to the recruiting and assessment of new employees that are governed by EEOC and Title VII regulations. Although these will generally come under the jurisdiction of your organization's personnel department and will seldom be the direct responsibility of the manager who

interviews occasionally, it is wise for anyone who interviews or conducts searches for potential employees to be aware of these regulations and guidelines.

Advertising for Applicants

The search for applicants, like the interview itself, must be free from
discriminatory practices or references. Only bona fide qualifications
for the job may be listed as prerequisites for applicants.

When recruiting applicants through an employment agency, it
is wise to send a notice to each agency you deal with, saying that you
will accept referrals regardless of race, color, religion, national origin,
or sex.

Help-wanted ads should not contain any unlawful restrictions.
Race or color can never be a bona fide job qualification. However, if
religion, sex, or national origin is a bona fide qualification, this can
be specified.

The EEOC has ruled that placing job advertisements in separate
"male" and "female" columns in the help-wanted section violates the
Civil Rights Law unless sex is a bona fide occupational qualification
(e.g., in the case of models for women's fashions). Most newspapers
have since set up columns titled "Male–Female," and the bulk of
employment advertising will fall in this neuter listing.

Testing Guidelines

It is not enough to use tests that are "professionally developed." The
EEOC says employers should use a total personnel assessment system
that is nondiscriminatory, placing special emphasis on the following:

Select appropriate tests after analyzing jobs to determine essential
job requirements.

Hire qualifiable applicants as well as those already qualified.

Conduct testing and interviewing of minority applicants with
personnel who are committed to equal employment opportunity policies.

Validate tests against job performance rather than by what they
claim to measure. They should be separately validated for
minorities.

Offer retesting to applicants who failed to achieve a passing score
but who have since had more training or related experience.

Documents and Records

It is also unlawful to require an applicant to submit certain records. In general, this includes any record or document which would provide the proof that the applicant is a member of a minority group. Included are birth certificates, naturalization papers, baptismal records, and preemployment photos. If a record or document would provide an answer to any one of the questions which have been determined illegal by the EEOC or Title VII, do not ask the applicant to submit it.

GUARDING AGAINST VIOLATIONS

In summary, then, both the organization as a whole and the individual interviewer bear the responsibility for nondiscriminatory hiring and interviewing practices. Good intentions are insufficient defense in discrimination suits; an illegal action, procedure, or question may be ruled as evidence of discrimination even if there was no intent to use information for discriminatory purposes.

The interviewer can guard against exposing his or her organization to a discrimination suit by taking the following precautions:

Examine your own biases and prejudices carefully, and scrupulously avoid bringing them into the interview or evaluation situation. If you find that you are unable, despite your efforts, to evaluate certain classes of minorities objectively, be honest. Admit that this is not your forte, and try to arrange it so that someone else interviews these candidates.

Familiarize yourself thoroughly with the letter and intent of the law. This includes the federal regulations and their interpretation and the additional laws and regulations within your own state or the state in which you are interviewing. A periodic review of the illegal questions in Figures 9.1–9.3 will help, but this alone is insufficient. The full extent of restrictions on hiring procedures is ultimately decided by the courts, because they interpret existing regulations at both the state and federal levels. Some states provide guidelines to the restrictions in their fair employment practices laws, and the EEOC occasionally issues guidelines; watch current *Report Bulletins* for the latest federal developments.

Develop clearly defined job specifications for the specific position for which you are interviewing as well as a list of desirable characteristics for the job family in question. Then be absolutely sure that your inquiries and decisions are related to the needs of the position. Remember, the law allows you to hire the best-qualified candidate for the job, *providing* your decision is based on job-related criteria. Consequently, should you be faced with a discrimination suit, questions will be considered suspect if they are not directly related to the predetermined needs of the job.

Keep careful records to document reasons for rejection of candidates, especially if they fall into one of the sensitive categories or classes covered by EEOC regulations. These records should state as specifically as possible which job requirements the candidate does not meet and what evidence you have for concluding that he or she does not meet them. If, for example, the candidate does not have a high enough energy level for the position, in your opinion, record specific examples from the interview that led you to make this evaluation. If you have decided that his prior experience in other jobs has been insufficient to qualify him for the available position, state specifically the types of experience he is lacking. Firmly established job specifications combined with clearly stated reasons why the candidate did not meet these specifications will go a long way toward proving that your rejection of a candidate was for reasons other than discriminatory hiring practices.

If an interviewer follows these guidelines and if he is deeply committed personally to equal employment practices and policies, he can be fairly certain that he is basing his employment recommendations on legal, job-related criteria rather than on the race, color, sex, age, creed, or national origin of the candidate.

Chapter 10
Interviewing
the College
Candidate

Of all interviewing situations, perhaps the one requiring the greatest patience and versatility on the part of the interviewer is the interview with the brand-new college graduate or, as is more often the case, the student who will be graduated at the end of the current school term. Interviews with college candidates are unique in many respects. Especially in screening interviews carried out in the campus setting, an interviewer is likely to encounter a wider variety of applicants than he could ever expect to encounter during a day of in-house interviewing. He will talk to a large number of very young persons, ranging from the highly sophisticated and self-assured to the naive and terrified. Their majors will vary from those in which the interviewer is specifically interested to those that are so far afield the interviewer may well wonder if he has received some other interviewer's schedule by mistake. Their job experience will often be minimal or nonexistent, making it difficult to find a background topic, apart from their college work, which can be examined in depth. Their age, language, or appearance may create a barrier between them and the interviewer. Add to this the fact that the campus interviewer may have to interview a very large number of these candidates in one day, perhaps for only 20 or 30 minutes each, and that he may have no information at all on any of the candidates before they walk into the interviewing cubicle, and it's little wonder that so many otherwise adept and confident interviewers would rather commit hari-kari than spend a day on campus!

Naturally, some of these problems are most evident during the campus screening phase and are alleviated somewhat by the nature of the selection process, by the time those who have passed the on-campus screening have been invited for an in-house interview. Even at this point, however, interviewing a new college grad can be a tricky and sometimes painful experience, especially for the manager who is accustomed to interviewing applicants with several years' experience in the business or industrial world.

THE CAMPUS SCREENING INTERVIEW

Mental Set of the Interviewer

Too often an interviewer will arrive on campus for a day or two of screening without the appropriate mental set. If the interviewer is not mentally ready to cope with the wide variety of candiates he will meet in a telescoped time frame, he is quite likely to find at the end of the day that he is unable to differentiate between those who show promise as prospective employees and those who do not. All will tend to run together in a blur. Even worse is the interviewer whose attitude is that all potential candidates must look and act as if they had worked for his company for several years and must exhibit a comparable level of knowledge about the business world. This interviewer, by relying on his biases and prejudices for a judgment, is quite likely to screen out many good candidates on the basis of their "differentness" or naiveté, while recommending an equal number of candidates who have an appropriate appearance and a sophisticated line of chatter but who may actually have less potential as prospective employees.

The first task, then, is for the interviewer to "get his head together" before he ever approaches the campus. Especially in the case of the manager who visits the campus only once or twice a year to interview, the interviewer needs to think about what he is likely to encounter there. There are a number of questions that can be reflected upon prior to the visit, so that the interviewer has at least prepared himself mentally for the variety of interview situations that may be awaiting him.

What will the students be like? It might be helpful for the interviewer to find out what sort of reputation the college or university has and what sorts of students it attracts if he does not already know. Are most of this school's students considered to be sophisticated? Is the campus atmosphere informal or formal? Is the school policy considered ultraconservative or is its reputation liberal? Is the curriculum highly structured, or do the students have a great deal of choice? Are students encouraged to take part-time jobs or participate in work-study programs, or are they urged to concentrate solely on academics? Are extracurricular activities encouraged or deemphasized? Is the school especially noted for technology, business, or liberal arts? The answers to all these questions will not only help the interviewer anticipate the kinds of students he will be most likely to see during the visit, but also enable him to spot more quickly any students that are unusual in any respect, as compared with their peers. Suppose, for example, that a particular campus has a reputation for being very liberal and exceedingly informal. The interviewer who is on his way to this campus for screening interviews might just as well resign himself to the fact that he is going to interview some students who have long hair, beards, blue jeans, and radical ideas. He would be wise to prepare himself mentally for these students, especially if he himself tends to be middle-aged, conservative, and the type of person who has always felt that an applicant should be clean-shaven, soft-spoken and deferential, and clad in a grey pin-striped suit and tie. With the proper forethought, perhaps he can repress his shudder when the bearded candidate walks in and get about the business of finding out what kind of young person is hidden under the beard. After all, if this type of appearance is the norm for this particular campus, then it stands to reason that both brilliant and mediocre candidates may appear in similar guises here—just as both brilliant and mediocre candidates may appear in expensive suits at an Ivy League school. By the same token, at the extremely liberal and informal school a candidate who is faultlessly dressed and formal, even though he may have more aesthetic appeal for the interviewer, might well be suspected of being a misfit in his particular surroundings. Thus it helps the interviewer to know as much as he can about the school and the types of students it attracts, so he can know what to expect.

What majors will the students have? Unless the interviewer has been assured ahead of time that he will only be interviewing business majors, or chemistry majors, or whatever he is specifically seeking, he would be wise to prepare himself mentally for encounters with students from every conceivable field of study. This is especially true if the interviewer represents a large corporation with a wide diversity of jobs; even if he himself is seeking only chemical engineers, he is likely to find on his schedule students who have majored in any field imaginable and who are interested in working for his company in some area over which he has no authority. This is also true, of course, for persons who are looking for candidates in sales, management training, or other areas which may not require a specific major field of study. And finally, any interviewer, no matter how specific the area of interest he and his company represent, is apt to find that a certain percentage of the students on his schedule have simply signed up for an interview with him by mistake. Regardless of the circumstances that have led to an interview with these students with the "wrong" major, the interviewer should be mentally prepared for them and mentally ready to talk with them intelligently and to listen to them perceptively. Perhaps they have good, logical reasons for wanting a position that seems at odds with their major, and the open-minded interviewer may arrive at the conclusion that this person may, after all, be a promising candidate for the job. Or perhaps the student may be educationally unqualified for the job in question but a superior candidate for a job elsewhere in the interviewer's organization—in which case the interviewer can do both his company and the student a favor by recommending the student to the person in charge of recruiting for this area of the organization. Even if a student is clearly in the wrong field and the interviewer has nothing at all to offer him, it is just good business to continue the interview rather than dismiss the candidate rudely. Who knows? Perhaps his roommate or his best friend is the top candidate in his graduating class and will be influenced by your treatment of his misguided friend.

The interviewer should also reflect on the wide variety of attitudes and degrees of sophistication he is likely to encounter and be prepared to deal with them appropriately. On the typical campus, students will run the gamut from those who are exceedingly knowledgeable about the world of work and about their chosen place in this world to those who have no idea what kind of job they might want or even what kinds might be available. It is not unusual for a campus recruiter to interview a senior who has had summer positions involving a great deal of responsibility in a field related to his major. This student may know exactly what type of position she is seeking, how her strengths and her education apply to this position, and in what ways she is specifically suited to the organization for which she is interviewing. She may, in fact, be able to tell the recruiter things about his company or his position that the recruiter himself didn't know! On the other hand, the very next senior the recruiter interviews may be totally naive about the ways in which he might use his major field of study once he has graduated. Perhaps he has never had a part-time or summer job, and often he has no idea how businesses and industries are structured. He simply does not know what to expect or even what he should strive for. This does not necessarily mean that the first candidate is more attractive than the second, but it does alert the interviewer to the fact that they will need to be handled differently during the course of the interview.

Finally, the interviewer should be aware that students differ vastly in their level of sophistication regarding the actual interview process. This may depend in part upon the extent of their experience in the world of work—a student who has held several responsible jobs and who knows what he or she wants will often come across as more "smooth" in the interview, but not always. Other factors may also be involved. The student who has already had 20 or 30 interviews this semester will probably appear much more at ease and more sophisticated than the student who is at his first interview, for example, regardless of their relative levels of knowledge and experience. And of course the personality of the individual student enters into the picture, too. Some are just born "smooth-talkers" who never appear flustered, while others will stammer and perspire their way through every interview no matter how much practice they have had.

In recent years, the greatest single factor affecting the sophistication of students in the interview situation has been the advent of courses which teach students how to interview. Students are actually coached and rehearsed on how to dress, how to speak, what questions are likely to be asked, and what answers they should give. These courses are commendable, up to a point, if they are mainly designed to help the candidate know what to expect and to increase his or her self-confidence. Unfortunately, though, many go further and actually try to teach the student to come across in the interview as something or someone he or she is not. Needless to say, these put the interviewer at a disadvantage unless he is extremely alert and adept, because he will find himself evaluating the student as he has been *taught to appear*, rather than as he actually is. Ultimately, of course, this type of interview-taking instruction also does a disservice to the student, who may well find himself hired for the wrong job on the basis of his less than genuine answers during the interview. The campus interviewer, then, should find out before he arrives on campus whether this particular institution offers such a course, and, if so, he should be alert for "coached" candidates. Ways in which these candidates may be dealt with were discussed in Chapter 8.

Preparation for the Campus Interview

It is usually impossible to prepare for a series of campus interviews with the same care one would use in preparing for an in-depth, in-house interview. Because the interviewer is a guest on campus, he generally has little or no control over the facilities or environment in which he will interview. Similarly, his schedule is generally set up for him, so that he has no voice in the matter of whom he will interview, at what time of day, or for how long. Perhaps the most annoying deterrent to preinterview planning is the absence of information on the candidate. Very seldom does the campus interviewer receive resumés or data sheets before he arrives on campus; the more usual practice is for him to receive all the sheets for the day's schedule upon his arrival for the interview. This, of course, makes it impossible for the interviewer to spend a quiet hour digesting the known information about the applicant and planning his specific interview objectives.

However, there are certain things a campus interviewer can do to minimize these problems. Take the matter of facilities, for example. He usually has no choice as to where he will interview, and the rooms that are assigned visiting interviewers often tend to be bleak, practically barren little cubicles. But even so, the interviewer can probably maneuver the chairs so that a desk or table does not form a barrier between him and the candidate. He can determine ahead of time whether coffee for himself and his applicants is available and find out where the applicant's coat should be hung. He may even want to carry along his own "Do Not Disturb" sign for posting on the door during interviews. He can make sure, before the first candidate arrives, that there is an ashtray available (if smoking is permitted in the building), that the chairs and table are not dust-covered, and that the Muzak, if any, is turned down. Of course, on many campuses these details are handled by efficient placement directors or their secretaries, and the interviewer will not have to be bothered with them.

If a large number of students have signed up to interview with a particular interviewer while he is on campus, the placement director may try to convince him to lengthen the day's schedule—running, say, from 7:30 to 6:00 with a half hour for lunch. Or, he may be asked to shorten interviews from a half hour to 20 minutes. The interviewer should try very hard to resist this sort of pressure. After eight interviews or so, the average interviewer will find that he is running out of gas; from that point on, he will risk missing some good candidates or accepting some bad ones because he will be too tired to listen attentively or to pick up flags. As for 20-minute interviews, they are just too brief to accomplish much. To avoid getting into this situation, the interviewer who discovers that too many students wish to see him might call in another interviewer from his organization if it is located nearby. If not, he may want to stay another day, if his schedule permits, or promise to come back on another day in the near future.

When it comes to planning the interview itself, about the best the campus interviewer can do without prior information on an applicant is to keep firmly in mind the general traits and background he is seeking. An interviewer who is not a seasoned recruiter should prepare for a campus visit by getting a briefing from his organization's employment director, preferably focusing on the highest-level or largest divisions he is recruiting for. The briefing should include present or future openings for which certain exceptional candidates might qualify.

A profile of skills and characteristics which are desirable in these areas should be prepared. Personnel, management, technical employment, and sales could be broad areas in which to designate desirable skills and characteristics to serve as guidelines. Then some broad objectives can be formulated in keeping with these desired qualities.

From this point on, flexibility is the key, and each interview will have to be structured very quickly upon meeting the candidate and looking over his or her data sheet. Needless to say, this can best be handled by the interviewer who has the most concise idea of what he is looking for in a candidate, so that he can instantly assess the available data and formulate questions that will provide the missing, essential information.

Verification

As we have implied, the interviewer may well find that he gets his first glimpse at the data sheet or application when the candidate walks in the door for the interview and hands it over. Many interviewers become so flustered by this that they spend the remainder of the interview buried in the application, asking direct questions whose answers already appear there. Even if they know how to use the cone system, they feel thay haven't sufficient time or opportunity to formulate their objectives for the interview and then to frame their open-focus questions to get the cones started. As a result, they waste the interview and fail to establish a rapport.

When all the prior information on a candidate is withheld until the candidate appears, the best way to handle the situation is to spend the first few minutes of the interview on "verification." Verification is the process of going through the written data systematically with the applicant. The interviewer might say to the applicant, after the introductions have been completed: "I haven't had a chance to go over this. Could we run through it together?" Then the interviewer can look the information over briefly without appearing to be ignoring the candidate. He should ask any questions he has about dates, ask for brief clarification on points that aren't clear to him, and then set the application or data sheet aside. In just a minute or two with the data sheet, the interviewer should be able to pick up enough information to help him select two or three cones to run. Since he wants to use open-focus questions to start these cones, he will not need to remember specific dates or sequences from the data sheet; it will be sufficient if he remembers, say, that the applicant was active in student government, that he majored in American history, and that he has had a summer job in a state senator's office.

Keeping Track

Interviewers in campus situations often fear that they will be unable to keep track of the students they interview; that is, they feel they won't remember the strengths, weaknesses, or unique experience of any one student after interviewing ten others in the same day. As a result, they resort to furious note-taking, even if they generally conduct their in-house interviews without a notepad in sight. This, of course, spoils the climate of the interview and erects a communication barrier.

Even worse, some campus interviewers tape-record their interviews so they can play them back and make their notes later. This tactic is highly inadvisable, as it is certain to make a candidate nervous and reluctant to speak frankly or even to make him or her angry and defensive. Either way, a bad impression of your company is created.

The best solution we have found is this: If you are doing so many consecutive interviews that you cannot remember them all, keep a small tape recorder with you, and keep it tucked away (not turned on, please!) in your briefcase or a desk drawer. Then, when each applicant leaves the room, dictate a few brief notes to yourself before the arrival of the next applicant. As you become accustomed to this method, you will find that just a few key words set on tape will be sufficient to jog your memory about the outstanding features of each candidate. You could also briefly jot down these few notes on the bottom of the candidate's data sheet between interviews.

Between applicants, the interviewer may also want to rate the candidate on the various skills and characteristics that he has set up as desirable criteria for the broad employment areas within his organization. He can do this quickly and easily on an evaluation form similar to the one shown in Figure 7.2.

Application of the Cone System

The whole campus screening process is negated if it cannot be used to discern the candidates who fit the job as well as the organization from the ones who do not. Utilization of the cone system is an excellent way of assessing students quickly and keeping them straight in your mind, enabling you to later separate that student from the many others you have seen. Even if cones are begun with the same open-focus question for several consecutive students, their responses will be quite different, suggesting different paths for you to pursue through your moderate-focus questions and probes.

The cone system in the campus interview is very similar to the system as utilized in an in-depth interview, discussed in Chapters 6 and 7, except that there is likely to be less time to devote to this phase of the interview during campus screening and a smaller number of potential topics in which to run cones.

By the time the interviewer spends a couple of minutes breaking the ice in the introduction, a couple of minutes verifying data, perhaps half a minute laying out the structure of the interview, and 5–7 minutes for the influence and sell phase at the end of the interview, followed by a 2-minute summary and close, there is just not much time left in a 25- or 30-minute interview. At most, only 15–17 minutes can be programmed into three 5-minute cones, and that is a very good way to plan the campus screening interview.

The topics for the cones, of course, will be dictated by the background of the student as well as by the interviewer's objectives. If the student has had a lot of outside work experience, the interviewer may want to run one cone on educational experiences and the other two on the two most substantial jobs, such as summer employment in corporations similar to your own or experiences in co-op programs, where the student works for six months and then goes to college for six months. But many students have not held jobs other than, perhaps, part-time work that is not particularly applicable to their career plans or commensurate with their talents. With these students, the interviewer will probably have to select from among the following cones: undergraduate work, graduate work (if any), high-school activities, campus extracurricular activities, and part-time jobs. These part-time jobs, if they are not very significant, can all be covered in a single cone. Some students may also have had special experiences, such as Peace Corps, ROTC, military service, or ex-change study in another country which could serve as a topic for a cone.

In California, because of invasion of privacy laws, interviewers must be careful when inquiring into outside activities. The law states that such inquiries must be job-related. However, even in California, most college students are anxious to talk about their activities on campus, especially if they've had a leadership role. So the college student is not as sensitive to potential violations of the privacy law as are entry-level applicants under other circumstances. In any event, try, if you run an outside activity cone, to connect it very closely with the student's college experiences and with the work that he or she is being considered for. Attempt to relate the student's experiences to the established characteristics of the job family for which you are attempting to hire, and avoid pressing the student to discuss activities if he seems reluctant to elaborate on the nature or extent of his involvement.

One other modification may be necessary in the cone system during campus screening, either because of the limited time available or the inexperience of the candidate. This modification is the use of more moderate-focus questions at the top of the cone in favor of wide open ones. In other words, the interviewer might say: "I see you majored in mathematics. Could you discuss some of your work in that field?" This is more moderate than the alternative, "Tell me about your education," and helps to utilize the time efficiently by guiding the candidate toward the area in which the interviewer really needs information.

The following dialogue from an actual campus screening inter-view illustrates the modification of the cone system to get at some of the accomplishments, attitudes, and career goals of a liberal arts senior. In this instance, the recruiter was representing a large cor-poration with potential positions for college graduates in a wide variety of areas. Let's look in on his interview to see how he structures the situation to learn some of the candidate's strengths and weaknesses, preferences, and career goals. In a very brief interview and with little actual job experience in the candidate's background to go on, he is able to learn quite a bit about her that will enable him to determine what department within his company she might wish to work in and whether he should recommend her to this department for further consideration in the form of a location visit.

We will join the interview just after the introductory phase, at the beginning of the structure phase, and proceed through the assessment phase.

INT: As you know, I have a data sheet here, and I've had a chance to look it over quickly. I'd like to take the next few minutes to ask you some questions about your background and your studies, and then I'd certainly like to give you a chance to ask me any questions you have about our organization and our possible openings. How does that sound?

APP: Just fine.

INT: Good. Maybe we could start out by your telling me a little about your major field of study. I understand it was psychology. I wonder if you could tell me, just briefly, about some of your work in that discipline.

APP: Okay. Actually I majored in psychology and minored in sociology, and in a sense the class I enjoyed most was a combination of both psychology and sociology. It was social psychology. I found that my instructor was very stimulating, which in turn made the course content stimulating for me, and I found I worked very hard in this class as a result. I also enjoyed abnormal psychology, because this dealt with many of the conditions that you find prevalent in mental institutions, and this material was also interesting and challenging to me. Other than that, there was no particular single course that I could cite that was especially interesting—just the entire area of psychology.

INT: That sounds very interesting. Now, I wonder if we might move over just a bit, and you could tell me about your minor field.

APP: I minored in sociology which, as I progressed, became increasingly interesting, because you can relate things you learn in this field directly to things that are happening in the community. At one point I did wish I had majored in sociology, but it was easy to combine sociology and psychology to come up with courses that are going to help me achieve my goal of helping people and contributing to the community.

INT: You say at one time you thought maybe you should have majored in sociology. How do you feel about that now?

APP: Well, I am happy with my decision to remain in psychology, because I have discovered that my professional interests are more in line with a degree in psychology. My interests in sociology can always be satisfied in other ways, such as through reading; so I believe I made the right decision.

INT: In your minor field of sociology, could you describe some of the experiences you enjoyed?

APP: My favorite subjects, because I could really get into the meat of them, were social stratification and race relations. These were courses that were really dynamite. I had a chance to get involved and to learn a few things about myself as well as about things happening in the outside world. Social stratification gave me a lot of information about the set-up and the organization of society, which was very useful in understanding the sorts of things that are happening in the world.

INT: You used the word "dynamite." Could you elaborate on what you mean by this?

APP: By that, I meant that I feel exhilarated with the material being presented and almost compelled to seek more information in these areas on my own, on things that I had just gotten a smattering of information about during the class. So it was dynamite in the sense that it pushed me to learn more and develop my interests further.

INT: Well, it sounds as if you were very interested in some of your studies. Had you given any thought to continuing in either of these disciplines, once you get your bachelor's degree?

APP: Yes, I hope to continue in psychology, but I haven't quite decided which direction to take. I think I would like to go into some form of personnel work and develop from there. Eventually, I believe I might like to work in the area of equal employment, helping a company to recruit and place minority persons in the right jobs. I would like to find a combination of work experience and part-time study, perhaps at night, so that I can learn from my actual work experience where my studies should be leading me.

INT: Well, you might be interested to know that our organization has a fine educational continuation program, which allows people to go on for advanced degrees while they are on the job. If you like, I'll give you a brochure on it.

APP: Yes, this is something I am very interested in.

INT: Well, I think from what you've told me that I have a pretty good feeling for your work in these major and minor fields of study. I would be most interested now in pursuing the part-time work that you did on campus. Could you tell me about that?

APP: Certainly. I worked at the registrar's office for about a year. It wasn't a very responsible position; I simply filed student records and transcripts. But I had a number of other part-time jobs while I was going to school. I worked as a salesperson in a large department store here in town and did some typing for a private business firm. I worked in a factory on an assembly line on the early morning shift for a while. The last job I had was with our city's foster homes project. This was a pilot project involved with placing supposedly impossible-to-place juveniles in foster homes. I did some collating and compilation of test scores for them.

INT: Of all these jobs, was there any one in particular that might have turned you on?

APP: Yes, the one with the foster homes project, because it tied in with my field of study. My own work was pretty routine, since I was just part-time clerical help, but I was able to see what they were doing, and I was very interested in the outcome. The children themselves were all emotionally disturbed and this project was giving psychological tests to potential foster parents. I think the major premise was that by very closely screening and working with the parents and matching them up with the kids ahead of time, these children would be more likely to stay in the homes than if they were just placed in any clean home where the family had good intentions to keep foster children. So this was extremely interesting.

INT: It sounds very interesting. Could you fill me in on your reasons for leaving that job?

APP: Yes, unfortunately I had to leave the project when my course schedule conflicted with the working hours during second semester. In fact, I had so many hours of class this semester that I decided not to take a part-time job at all, except for some evening baby-sitting jobs. But I was very disappointed to give the job up, because I was so interested in the project.

This was different from quitting my other part-time jobs in order to juggle my schedule or seek higher-paying work; I didn't mind leaving those other jobs so much, because they were rather boring in the sense that they were totally unrelated to my studies or my interests.

INT: Well, you certainly had a wide range of part-time jobs. I imagine you were able to contribute quite a bit to your school expenses by working so hard.

APP: Yes, I think overall, counting summer jobs, I was able to earn about 40 percent, and my parents were able to pay the rest; so I was fortunate.

INT: That's very commendable. You mentioned summer jobs. Could you fill me in on these, or were these some of the work you have already mentioned?

APP: Oh, I forgot to mention my summer job when we were discussing the work I did during the school year. For several summers, I was employed by the high school to baby-sit for children whose parents were enrolled in extension courses at the school. That was fun.

INT: Well, you have certainly given me a complete rundown of your many jobs, and it sounds like you had a great variety of experiences. Now I wonder if we might discuss very briefly some of your outside activities while you were in college.

APP: Certainly. Most of my time was spent with one organization, the Black Studies program, whose main objective was to promote more courses in black history on our campus—more studies that we felt related to the needs and experiences of black people in the United States. I was very active in this.

INT: How did you feel about this program?

APP: I felt it was good and necessary. I felt needed, and also I felt that I needed the program; so it was very satisfying all around. In many instances it was frustrating, yet it made me feel better for having done something other than just sitting back and saying "This situation is terrible."

INT: Could you expand on the ways in which it was frustrating, and what you did to counteract this frustration?

APP: Well, it was frustrating to the extent that we tried to institute many changes on the campus or to institute many new courses that never materialized because other people did not understand why these changes or courses were desirable. But we kept trying. We would talk to different people about our needs if we met with a dead end in one place, and we would try to marshall new facts and methods of persuasion to support our views. We really didn't expect instant success, because the concept of black studies was fairly new on campus, and we have a reasonably small percentage of blacks in decision-making capacities. But I do think some of the things we did resulted in some positive changes in the institution, even though we didn't always succeed.

INT: How did you accomplish these changes?

APP: Well, we used a rather direct approach. We initiated conferences with the president and with the heads of the various departments in which we believed a wider variety of classes should be offered. We presented to them what we felt were very logical and carefully researched reasons for whatever it was we wanted changed or for the courses we desired them to institute. We never sponsored demonstrations or any kind of disruptive activity, because we felt that at this particular school these activities would cause us to lose the respect of the faculty. But we often did use petitions as a means of demonstrating how many students were interested in the courses or activities we advocated. These petitions were usually presented at the time of our personal visit to the official in question, because we found that personal communication was usually more effective than any other method.

INT: It sounds as if you were quite busy with this activity. Were you involved in any other extracurricular activities?

APP: Yes, I was quite active with the Business and Professional Women's Club on campus. We did various projects such as giving baskets to the needy at Christmas and working with disadvantaged children. Mostly we acted as "big sisters" to children whose parents were unable to provide them with educational experiences. We each adopted a "little sister," and we took them to places such as the zoo, the art institute and museums, and into our homes for the day to give them different kinds of exposure and experiences.

INT: How did you feel about this?

APP: I felt it was very worthwhile for the children, and also for me personally. For one thing, it was very ego-satisfying, and you developed a great deal of attachment to the girl you happened to be working with. I found myself actually treating her as a younger sister and doing things for her outside the scope of the project—taking her to movies, buying her clothes and toys, and so on. I felt I was definitely a better person for having participated in this project, and I believe I helped my "little sister" as well.

INT: I'm sure that's true. Now, I would just like to ask . . . in all that you have told me, I notice a recurring theme. You seem to be very interested in studying about and working with children—especially children who are disadvantaged or who are mentally or emotionally disabled. Have you considered this interest as a possible basis for a career?

APP: Yes, I did at one time. But recently, my career interests have shifted more toward working with adults, to help them make the most of their potential and to find their own niche in society. I think a lot of this change in my thinking has been prompted by my work in the Black Studies program as well as by some of the classes I have enjoyed, such as social stratification. So at present, I believe I am leaning toward some sort of personnel work, especially in a job which would enable me to help minorities find suitable employment. I think this is the best way in which I can fulfill my own goals, while utilizing my training in psychology and sociology to the best advantage.

Pitfalls for the Campus Recruiter

Campus recruiting is perhaps the most difficult form of interviewing because the time is so short, the workload so heavy, and the atmosphere so strange to many interviewers. However, many of the most common pitfalls can be avoided by taking the following precautions.

It is essential for the right kind of person to do college recruiting—one who is not easily shocked or put off by the outward appearance or surface characteristics of the students and one who has kept in touch with the campus scene. The recruiter who has not been on a college campus for ten years or so should be briefed by someone within the organization who has had more recent and closer contact with the campus. He should plan to arrive on campus the day before his interviews to walk around and see what is going on and what appears to be the "norm" in this environment. Perhaps he could meet with the placement director on campus to get a briefing before beginning his interviews or have lunch or dinner with a faculty member to get a picture of the campus atmosphere.

Many campus interviewers try to conduct their interviews without any idea of the students' study program. If you are to spend a day interviewing engineers, get a catalog from the engineering school ahead of time and look over the curriculum. Then you won't have to ask questions about the basic course requirements in the field. You can spend more time on the attitudes the candidates have about the courses they took, and you will know whether they are referring to snap courses or difficult ones.

Cooperation and communication with the placement office is essential. Literature on your own organization should be sent to this office early for distribution; more candidates on campus are studying such literature prior to interviews these days. Determine whether the placement office coaches and prepares its candidates. In some schools, students have even been rehearsed on videotape or closed-circuit television in role-playing interview situations. If you know this ahead of time, you can judge how sophisticated your candidates are likely to be.

Because the time for each interview is so short, it is difficult to use it to the best advantage. Therefore, an interview plan is essential. Time must be managed wisely, and the interviewer must not allow herself to be diverted from her planned objectives.

Many interviewers talk too much in campus interviews. They mistakenly believe that their biggest job is one of public relations; they talk about themselves, their company, and the job, rather than encourage the student to provide information about himself or to ask questions. This, of course, gives the student the impression that the interviewer is uninterested in him as well as prevents the interviewer from obtaining valuable information. The interviewer should not talk any more than 50 percent of the time overall, and during the assessment phase the student should be allowed to predominate.

Because of time limitations, many interviewers fail to break the ice properly in the campus setting. The introductions are too stilted. They do not get on a first-name basis, tell the student what company they represent, or find out what the student prefers to be called. In short, they fail to put the student at ease.

Applicants who have been coached or who have had a great deal of practice because of the number of prior interviews they have had can cause the campus interviewer to greatly overevaluate them. One problem is that they have heard the same questions over and over and are prepared for them. A major benefit of the cone system is that it helps overcome this advantage. Although the student may be familiar with the open-focus question at the top of the cone, the interviewer who listens properly and focuses on what the student is saying can develop the cone into a very nondirective exploration of the subject, making it impossible for the student to use programmed or memorized answers. Chapter 8 contains more tips for handling the coached or practiced applicant.

Interviewers must avoid giving advice and counseling during the campus interview. Sometimes a student will try to manipulate the interview by asking, "Please give me some tips on how to be more effective in selling myself." The interviewer who succumbs to this ploy will find at the end of the interview that he or she has gathered very little information about the applicant. All too often, the student asks the question precisely to avoid being questioned about other subjects. But if the student appears to be honestly seeking advice, the interviewer should advise him or her to see the counselor in the placement office for help.

Too many interviewers on campus make hasty decisions on the basis of surface factors; that is, they get turned off early in the interview by a student whose appearance does not come up to their standards, for example, or turned on by the halo effect created by a practiced sophisticated applicant. This is where it pays for the interviewer to be acutely aware of his or her own biases and prejudices and to try to set them aside in order to objectively evaluate the whole individual.

Often, because of lack of time, the student leaves with a feeling that his needs for information have not been met. No matter how short the time, be sure you answer any relevant questions the student may have about the job or the organization. (Irrelevant questions, such as "How do you like your job?", should be sidestepped.)

It is important to treat candidates fairly in order to preserve your organization's image on campus. Interviewers who take an ego trip by inducing stress, putting students into situations in which they have no experience, do inestimable harm to their organization's public image on campus. So do those who dismiss the unsuitable candidate too abruptly or too early in the interview. Remember, if candidates are disgruntled after their interview, they are likely to spread the word about their ill treatment around the campus. Some excellent candidates have been known to boycott corporations whose recruiters have established the reputation of rudeness to students.

LOCATION VISITS

Once the campus screening interviews have been accomplished, the interviewer will be responsible for selecting those candidates who have passed the initial screening and who appear to be suitable candidates for positions within the organization. These students will then be invited for a location visit, that is, a trip to the organization offices so that others within the company can get a better look at them and where they, in turn, can learn more about the organization.

To Invite or Not to Invite?

If the interviewer has kept good track of her many candidates during the days she has spent on campus and if she had her objectives and desirable characteristics firmly in mind during the interviews as well as while she was rating each candidate at the close of the interview, she will be able to determine which are most deserving of a closer look. When she gets back on the plane to go home, she will be equipped to rank the candidates she has seen on campus or at least to assign them to three or four categories—excellent prospects, good prospects, marginal, and unsuitable, for example. Even more important, she will know *why* her top candidates are in the top bracket, what they have to offer, and how they compared with others who will be politely turned down with a thank-you letter.

There is no cut-and-dried rule governing the number of candidates or the percentage of the candidates who should be invited for location visits. This depends in part, of course, on the number of positions you expect to fill from these candidates, the total number screened on campus, the calibre of the candidates you interviewed, and the amount of money your organization is willing to spend on location visits. Some interviewers habitually invite too few. They extend invitations for location visits only to "superstar" applicants. This selectivity causes them to miss many potentially good candidates who may have been reasonably impressive but not spectacular in the initial screening. In addition, of course, the "superstars" will be pursued by many companies and organizations; so your own organization may end up losing them with no other alternative candidates to fall back on. On the other hand, an even greater number of companies invite too many candidates for on-site interviews, including all the marginally acceptable applicants as well as those they are really interested in. A happy medium must be reached, so that the number of candidates invited is sufficient to fill your needs, allowing for those who will inevitably choose positions elsewhere, but not so large that time and money are wasted in looking at students who stand very little chance of being offered a job.

If there are candidates you are just not sure about—and there will be many following a series of brief screening interviews—perhaps you could compromise by seeing the candidate again at an intermediate location. If your office is in Los Angeles, say, and the candidate is in Boston, you may well hesitate to spend the company's money to fly her across the country if you are unsure whether she meets specifications or not. But perhaps you could easily invite her to visit your regional office on the East Coast so that a couple of other managers could meet her, or you could ask one of your colleagues who will be in Boston to have lunch with her before making the final decision about the invitation to the home office.

Some Pitfalls on Location

In general, interviewing a college student on location is pretty much like any other form of in-depth interviewing. However, there is a great tendency to overwhelm the college candidate. Typically, she will only be there for a day or so, and quite a few people within your organization may want to meet her—especially if she is under consideration for positions in more than one area. Some will tend to drill her with too many questions. Others will try to give her the "hard sell" on your organization. All this can be pretty confusing and upsetting for the college student, who is nervous and impressed with the importance of making a good impression to begin with.

It is a good idea to set a schedule for the visiting candidate ahead of time and to try to determine who will talk with her about what. It is not necessary for everyone who interviews her to ask the same questions about her educational background, for example, nor is it necessary for everyone to sell her on the organization. It is far easier on the student, as well as less repetitious and boring, if the topics of investigation are divided up among the interviewers according to their areas of interest or expertise and notes compared later, after the student has gone. Of course, all those who will meet with the student should be briefed ahead of time by the campus recruiter who recommended her, so that they will be aware of what was learned during the campus screening interview.

There is no doubt that college recruiting is difficult and time-consuming and that it requires excellent interviewing and management skills. But it continues to be one of the best and most popular ways of obtaining young people for entry-level professional, technical, and premanagement positions who can be trained from the start according to your own organization's methods and structure. Without a doubt, the art of campus recruiting is an art well worth mastering.

Chapter 11
Various Forms of the Selection Interview

Much of the material in the preceding chapters has concerned the in-depth interview—for example, the type that might be used by a manager to make a hiring decision or a recommendation for a hiring-decision interview on a professional, technical, or managerial candidate. This is especially true of the discussion of evaluation in Chapter 7, because the depth of communication we suggested in this chapter would probably not be possible in a brief interview with, say, an inexperienced applicant for routine clerical work. We have also dealt exclusively with the interview as a one-on-one situation in which a single interviewer and a single candidate are involved.

In this chapter, we will discuss other forms of the selection or employment interview, including those where an in-depth approach will be either unwarranted or impossible, and those involving more than two participants.

SCREENING INTERVIEWS

The screening interview differs from the in-depth interview in that it is generally, as its name implies, a preliminary interview. It is used primarily to weed out clearly unacceptable candidates in a situation where there are a great number from which to choose, so that the "possibilities" can be passed along for further interviewing in greater depth. Although the screening interview does not seek the detailed knowledge desired in a hiring-decision interview, it still requires a certain amount of meaningful communication if the screening is to be accurate.

Of course, a screening interview can be used as the first step in assessing candidates for any type of job at any level. It is frequently utilized in college recruiting, for instance. (We have already discussed this rather specialized form of screening interview in Chapter 10.) Generally, however, screening interviews are concentrated on entry-level positions or in hiring unskilled or lower-level workers. Typical positions in which the screening interview is common include production-line workers, file clerks, unskilled hospital employees or construction workers, and so forth.

In our discussion of the screening interview, we will emphasize the adaptations of the communication system and of the cone system to accommodate these entry-level and unskilled workers. For screening interviews involving professional candidates, of course, these adaptations would not be necessary, and the techniques outlined elsewhere in the book for in-depth interviews can be simply modified to fit the amount of time available and the type of evaluation desired.

The Entry-Level Candidate

The screening interview with the entry-level or unskilled candidate is probably the most difficult of all interviews to conduct. Often the candidate for entry-level jobs is extremely difficult to communicate with, especially for a fairly sophisticated interviewer. The candidate is likely to be recently out of school; he may have a very limited education; his verbal skills may be severely limited; and he is likely to have little practice in interviewing.

In addition, the entry-level candidate often is unsure what type of work he desires or even what type he is qualified for. This means that the interviewer must spend a great deal of time in ferreting out the qualifications the applicant may have, so that placement can be arranged in an area that will utilize the applicant's strengths and minimize his weaknesses.

To add to the interviewer's problems, the entry-level applicant may have never held a job before, and he is likely to have few outside activities. This makes it difficult for the interviewer to select topics for his cones and to find areas to probe in order to get at work-related attitudes.

Finally, if this type of applicant does have previous work experience, he often has rather poor employment records, including numerous positions of short duration. He may also have been fired or laid off from a series of positions. Of course, a somewhat suspect employment record increases the difficulty and challenge for the interviewer.

Preparing for the Screening Interview

Many interviewers seem to hold the opinion that, at the entry level or when unskilled applicants are involved, they can handle the screening process without much prior knowledge of the specific job or the job environment. This is a special problem because most screening at the entry level is done by employment representatives or personnel department employees who have little firsthand knowledge of the type of job in question. These are the interviewers who are likely to find themselves in the most trouble in the interview and at a loss when it comes to deciding whether the applicant should be screened out or recommended for further consideration.

As in most interview situations, the first step for the interviewer is to review the job specifications. When the employment representative receives the job requisition from the line manager, he should set up a meeting with this individual to discuss the particular needs of the job. He should interview the line manager to find out what he really has in mind for this kind of job and use the resulting data to fill out a job specification sheet such as those discussed in Chapter 4.

For instance, an employment representative for a large pharmaceutical manufacturer might determine that new employees for the packing operations on the company's production line should be able to stand for long periods in one place. They will work in close proximity to others. They must have a great deal of finger dexterity. They must work under some pressure, because the line moves steadily and rapidly. And they must have a strong feeling for quality control, because they will be dealing with pharmaceutical products.

These, then, would be characteristics the interviewer would want to look for in the screening interview. He would want to find out, for example, whether the applicant had ever performed a type of work which required standing still for long periods, how he felt about this aspect of the job, whether he could physically and mentally tolerate the continual standing combined with the repetitious nature of the work, whether he had ever had to keep pace with a production line or performed a similar job in which the pace created pressure, and so forth.

Entry-Level Communication Problems

Probably the greatest problem in the entry-level screening interview is the establishment of communication. Often the interviewer has failed to allow enough time for this type of interview. As a result, he rushes through the introductory phase of the interview without establishing a good rapport with the candidate. This problem is exacerbated by the limited communication skills brought to the interview by so many entry-level applicants. Their lack of extensive education, limited vocabulary, and unfamiliarity with the interview situation may combine to complicate communication. Of course, these problems are not common to all entry-level candidates, and some may be every bit as articulate and anxious to communicate freely as the interviewer himself.

The first step in the interview with the noncommunicative or ill-at-ease candidate, of course, is to make him or her feel comfortable. The introductory phase of the screening interview, then, is especially important. If this phase is rushed or improperly handled, there is little chance that a common ground for communication will be found.

The interviewer will want to begin by drawing the candidate into conversation. This initial conversation needn't be job-related; the important criterion is that it should focus on a topic which will make the applicant relax and open up. Anything that seems of interest to the candidate will do, providing it isn't an area that is likely to be sensitive or controversial.

Once a conversation has been successfully initiated, the interviewer will want to try to develop some understanding of and empathy for the individual. This is often very difficult when the two participants are from widely diverse backgrounds or educational levels. It is the job of the interviewer to try to assess the level at which the applicant is able to communicate and to bring himself down to that level if necessary, so that he will be clearly understood during the remainder of the interview. This may necessitate modifying his own vocabulary, simplifying the concepts and questions he plans to cover in the body of the interview, or both. The important task is to adjust the subject matter in such a way that the applicant can easily relate to it and then to be certain that the interviewer's actual wording and phraseology facilitate, rather than hinder, smooth communication.

On the other hand, some interviewers go overboard, with the result that they seem to be "talking down" to the applicant. Oversimplification or patronization can be even worse than erring in the other direction, because it can easily embarrass or insult the applicant. The best approach is to begin communicating slowly using your normal vocabulary and to modify your level of communication if and when you realize that the applicant is having trouble grasping either your wording or your concepts.

The interviewer should also listen carefully in these early phases of the interview for clues to the applicant's sensitivity to the needs of the interviewer, degree of relaxation, ability to organize thoughts, and general readiness to proceed into the body of the interview.

For some reason, in these exploratory moments early in the interview, many interviewers query the applicant about his or her education. This very often proves to be a sensitive area and thus an unfortunate opening choice with the entry-level or unskilled applicant. Perhaps the candidate has not finished high school, or his grades were questionable; perhaps, as an average or below-average student, he simply had unpleasant experiences during his formal schooling. As a result, defensiveness concerning educational background arises in many cases. Like other areas of sensitivity, this should be avoided in the early part of the interview in favor of other topics that the candidate is more likely to want to talk about.

Because so many applicants at this level seem to arrive at the interview with a defensive attitude, some positive "stroking" may have to be done from time to time to build the candidate's confidence. This may be accomplished by complimenting the applicant on a past achievement or by saying almost anything nice about him or her, as long as the compliment is sincere.

A poor climate is also created if the interviewer conveys the attitude that he holds the strings to the job and that the candidate must try to take the job away from him. This attitude serves only to increase anxiety and build greater defensiveness. It should be replaced by an attitude of concern for the individual and a genuine wish to discover whether he is the right person for the job and whether the job is right for him.

Sometimes applicants at this level turn out to be uncommunicative for reasons the interviewer cannot guess. For instance, one employment interviewer who took part in an interviewing training session was having difficulty establishing a rapport with a young woman who was applying for a clerical job. Whenever possible, she answered only "yes" or "no." The interviewer tried to open a cone on previous education, and the candidate clearly did not wish to discuss this topic. He tried to encourage her to talk about some of her favorite subjects in school, but she was not willing to volunteer much information. Since she had not held any jobs, he was somewhat at a loss as to what to pursue next. When he opened up the subject of outside activities, she refused to say anything about her outside interests, telling him she didn't feel they were job-related. Needless to say, both the interviewer and the applicant felt uncomfortable for the duration of the interview.

Afterward, the instructor of the training session, who had been monitoring the interview, talked with the applicant at length. He discovered that her husband had coached her on how to take the interview. Apparently the husband had recently completed a basic course in management which touched on interviewing and thus felt qualified to dispense advice. He told his wife to talk as little as possible, because interviewers don't like applicants who are too verbose. Even more important, he said, don't let them trick you into talking about your outside activities, because they try to use this as a vehicle to get you to say too much and then they hold what you say against you.

Obviously, the applicant had this advice on her mind during the interview and was naturally uncommunicative. But many entry-level candidates feel similarly uncomfortable under similar circumstances whether or not they have been coached, correctly or incorrectly, by a husband who has had a management course. It is up to the interviewer to try to detect the cause of the discomfort and to alleviate it, so that an atmosphere conducive to the free flow of communication can be established.

Modifying the Cone Approach

When using the cone system for entry-level interviewing, the interviewer will usually find that adaptations in the system, as presented in Chapter 6, will be necessary. This is necessitated by the somewhat limited comprehension abilities and communication skills exhibited by many entry-level applicants as well as the time limitations of most screening interviews.

The basic modification to consider is the way in which cones are initiated. With this type of applicant, it does not always work to open the cone with a completely open-focus question. The applicant simply fails to comprehend what is expected, and total silence is too often the result. The answer to this dilemma is to begin the cone a little farther down with a moderate-focus question related to information acquired from the application blank. For instance, instead of starting the cone with "Tell me about your last job," the interviewer might moderate his focus by beginning as follows: "I noticed you worked for the QRX Company on your last job. Maybe you could start out by describing some of your duties there, beginning with your arrival at work in the morning and taking me right through a typical day."

This kind of question gives the candidate a frame of reference, so that he has a better idea what sort of response is expected of him. In addition, it has the advantage of saving precious interview time by structuring the question to obtain the sort of information the interviewer needs, rather than leaving it so open that the applicant can waste time relating totally irrelevant details.

If this moderated question is still too broad for the candidate to handle, it can be narrowed down still further without deteriorating into direct questioning. For example, the interviewer could ask the applicant to describe what he does upon his arrival at work to set up his job station for the day and then proceed to inquire about successive steps in the work sequence.

It is usually wise to do some structuring in this sort of interview prior to beginning the body of the interview. Remember, candidates at this level are not apt to be as "interview-wise" or experienced as applicants at higher levels. During the structuring phase, the interviewer might tell the applicant: "One of the purposes of the interview is to try to get some feeling for you as a person and to determine what your strengths and talents are, so it will be possible to match you with a job within our organization. I'd like to start out by having you tell me something about your recent job with the PQR Company."

Another approach for beginning the body of the interview is to ask: "Of all the part-time jobs you've had, which one really turned you on?" Then, when you get a positive reply, you might say: "Well, could you just describe for me a day or so of that particular job, starting with when you went to work in the morning? Just casually tell me some of the things you actually did, how they trained you for that job, or anything else you would care to tell me about the job."

If this approach works, the interviewer can move on down the cone from there, gathering more detail about the applicant's attitudes and skills, likes and dislikes, relationships with others in the company, and so forth.

It should be stressed that the body of the interview, whether it consists of modified cones or of any other type of questioning, will simply not work if the candidate is insufficiently warmed up during the introductory phase or if the interviewer attempts to rush him through the information-gathering stage. This is what happened in the following excerpt from an interview with an applicant for a truck-driving job:

> INT: Ray, I understand you've spent most of your life in this city. I don't live in this area, but I think it's beautiful, with the mountains and all. There must be lots of outdoor activities. What do you do in your spare time?
>
> APP: Uh . . . (silence)
>
> INT: Are you a sportsman?
>
> APP: Uh . . . I'm . . . uh . . . sometimes I hunt.
>
> INT: I suppose this area is great for that. What do you hunt mostly around here?
>
> APP: Uh . . . deer.
>
> INT: I see. Do you enjoy any other outdoor activities? (pause) Skiing, or snowmobiling, or anything like that?
>
> APP: Uh . . . I tried skiing . . . couldn't stand up.
>
> INT: Yeah, I know what you mean. Neither can I. Well, let's talk a little bit about your job experience. I notice, in looking at your data sheet, that you've spent some time with the Air Guard. How did you happen to get involved in that, and what did you do in that job?
>
> APP: Well, my neighbor worked there . . . (pause) . . . he talked me into joining.
>
> INT: Do I understand correctly that you were a full-time employee there?
>
> APP: Uh-huh.
>
> INT: And could you describe the nature of your work there?
>
> APP: Fuel truck driving.
>
> INT: I see. Could you tell me a little about your training for this work? (pause) How did you learn to drive a fuel truck?
>
> APP: I trained at Chanute Air Force Base.

By revising the tempo of the interview and doing some additional warming up, the interviewer in this situation was finally able to get the applicant to communicate, at least to a limited extent. Later in the interview, the applicant actually made the following statement: "Well, when I was at Chanute, they taught us how to drive all kinds of trucks. Mostly I trained on a 5000-gallon tanker. It was an automatic shift, but we had others with six gears. They taught us about different kinds of fuels, about safety, quality control, stuff like that."

Obviously, the interviewer had succeeded in improving the climate for communication.

Occasionally, the process of communicating just never seems to get off the ground with the most reticent and noncommunicative interviewees, despite the best efforts of the interviewer. In fact, one of the most common complaints among interviewers is the following: "I just can't get entry-level people to talk. I've been trained in interviewing, I think I ask the right questions in the right way, but nothing happens."

Here is an example of this type of situation:

INT: Could you tell me a little about your last job?
APP: (Stammer, stutter) . . . I don't understand.
INT: Well, just tell me a little about what you did in a typical day as a file clerk.
APP: Well, I filed . . . I guess.
INT: Can you describe what you did in a little more detail?
APP: Uh, I just filed all day.
INT: Well, what sorts of things did you file?
APP: Papers.
INT: Was there anything particularly interesting about your job?
APP: No, not really.
INT: How did you feel about your job?
APP: What do you mean?
INT: Well, what was it like to work there?
APP: It was okay.

The interviewer who encounters a candidate like the one in this example certainly deserves sympathy, but he must forge ahead as best he can. If he has very carefully tried to warm up the applicant in the early stages of the interview and is still unable to evoke any responses, he may have to do a little more stroking or positive reinforcing at this point. He might say: "Well, Marian, I'm sure you had some very good training on that last job—training that will make you more valuable to the next company that hires you. Of course, what we are trying to do here is to look at that training and see how it might fit into our company's situation. Now, in order for me to understand how this might work, I wonder if you could tell me a little more about what you did on that job and what it was like."

In attempting to modify open-focus questions so that they are moderate-focus, some interviewers err by jumping right into direct questioning. This, of course, tends to create an interrogative atmosphere which is just as unsavory to the entry-level applicant as to the management-level candidate. In either case, extensive direct questioning provokes defensiveness on the part of the applicant. The interviewer who finds himself trapped in the bottom of the cone should try to utilize the moderate-focus probe, as discussed in Chapter 6, to get back up into the middle of the cone until it is absolutely necessary to resort to direct questioning.

Sensitive Topics

At the entry level, in particular, there are many topics that are wisely avoided, either because of legal constraints on the types of questioning considered pertinent to the job or just because of the applicant's potential sensitivity to various topics.

Recently, the Equal Employment Opportunity Commission, on both the federal and in many cases the state level, has placed restraints on lines of questioning that are not job-related. These restraints were discussed more fully in Chapter 9, but they bear mentioning here because of their special implications for entry-level interviewing. In simplified terms, the EEOC believes that interviewers should not need to know details about the applicant's personal life unless these aspects of his life directly affect his ability to perform the job for which he is being considered. In a screening situation for entry-level or unskilled employment, this limits the interviewer pretty much to job-related, historical situations. (Most applicants for a production-line job, for instance, would be highly unlikely to participate in any outside activities that would have any direct bearing on their ability to fill bottles, or tighten bolts, or whatever the job may require. This, of course, is not the case at management or professional levels, where many kinds of experience gained through outside activities may be brought to bear upon the various aspects of the job, and questioning in these areas may be invaluable in helping the interviewer to assess and evaluate the candidate.)

Similarly, the interviewer must be very careful about investigating the applicant's previous union activities. It is easy for the unwary interviewer to violate National Labor Relations Board policies in this regard, especially if he or she resorts to direct questioning in this area. Of course, it is not in violation of policy if an applicant who is proud of his union involvement elects to talk about it in response to an open-focus question, but he should not be directly quizzed about such involvement.

We mentioned earlier the reluctance of many entry-level or unskilled applicants to discuss their former education because of poor records or unhappy experiences in this area. Fortunately, most jobs at this level do not require an extensive investigation of prior education. Generally, the applicant will have no special educational qualifications for the job, and his grades in his general secondary-school courses will have little or no bearing on his ability to do the work. Often the interviewer will find it more fruitful to gloss over past educational experiences and to investigate instead the applicant's desire to become involved in some sort of training, night courses, or so forth, that might help increase his or her employment skills in the future.

To reiterate, then, the interviewer who is screening entry-level or unskilled employees will find it safest to restrict his or her questioning to job-related situations or attitudes. Even here, communication may be difficult. A number of studies on entry-level people in the labor market have shown that it is not unusual for these applicants to be reluctant to talk about previous job experiences. As we mentioned before, this may stem from their unpleasant job experiences and from poor employment records which they try to cover up both on the application and in the interview. If this is the case, these individuals will naturally try to respond curtly and to supply as little data as possible when the interviewer gets into the area of previous job experiences, in order to avoid trapping themselves. To minimize sensitivity in this area, the interviewer should try to begin his or her questioning by asking the applicant to describe a job which has been pleasant or one on which he feels he performed admirably.

Counseling in the Screening Interview

Usually we tell interviewers that they really aren't counselors and they shouldn't try to counsel during the interview. But in some cases at the entry level, a minimal amount of counseling becomes essential. This is especially true when the applicant is an untrained, hard-to-place individual who has no idea how his skills could be used and perhaps has no idea what his skills, if any, are.

In such a situation, if the applicant has passed the initial screening and appears to be a prospect for some sort of employment, the interviewer may have to resort to a few counseling techniques in order to get a better idea of the applicant's likes and dislikes. The interviewer may, for instance, paint capsule summaries of some of the areas in which the company can use entry-level employees and sample the applicant's reaction to each of these areas.

Often the applicant will be reluctant to express any preference in response to this line of questioning. A frequent response is: "I don't really care, I just need a job." Here, the interviewer must say something such as: "Of course, we appreciate that, but we'd rather put you in an area where we can use your abilities and possibly an area that you'd enjoy working and training in, rather than get you into an area that you might not care about." Usually, the applicant will respond if he can be reassured that by expressing his preferences he is not limiting his chances to be employed. (It would not be honest, of course, to use this approach if, in fact, you have only one job available. In many screening situations, however, the interviewer is actually screening for several different types of entry-level jobs at once, and thus the employment of this counseling tactic can serve the purposes of both himself and the candidate.)

The following excerpt from an interview with a young woman who has been a part-time clerical worker in several offices illustrates how a little counseling can help the interviewer to determine the best use of the applicant's skills within the organization which has a wide variety of clerical openings.

INT: Well, Peg, you've certainly had some very good job experience. Now, suppose I said to you, "Peg, you can have any kind of job you want in our company as long as you feel qualified to do it." This is just a hypothetical situation, of course, but do you have any idea what type of job you'd choose?

APP: Uh, some kind of office work, I guess.

INT: Well, of course we use many kinds of office workers in our company. We have some people who mostly file all day, others who usually type and some who spend most of their time doing things like mimeographing and photocopying, for example. Which of these areas do you think might appeal to you?

APP: I wouldn't care, as long as I had a steady job.

INT: Well, we realize you need a job, but it would be nice if we could try to put you in the job that would be most pleasant for you and that would use your skills best. Now, you've tried a little bit of several kinds of office work. You did a lot of filing at one time. How do you think you would feel about doing this again?

APP: Uh . . . I could do it real well . . . if I had to.

INT: Well, let's say you could choose between filing all day and typing all day—which do you think you'd pick?

App: Probably typing. (pause) It isn't so boring, sometimes.

Int: You used to run a mimeograph sometimes, didn't you?

App: Yes. (pause) I liked that. I'd like to do that again.

Int: What did you especially like about it?

App: Well, I liked . . . uh . . . making stuff that was ready to be handed out at meetings and stuff. (pause) And I liked messing with the machine. I kinda like machines.

Int: Have you ever had a chance to run any other office machines? (silence) Like a Xerox, or an addressograph?

App: No.

Int: Do you think you might like to learn to run other machines?

App: Oh, yes, I would. That would be interesting.

Although this type of mini-counseling is often difficult to do, the results are well worth the effort if it facilitates placement of an applicant in a position where that applicant will be happy, perform well, and perhaps learn new skills which will enable the company to promote him or her to a more responsible position in the future.

TEAM INTERVIEWS

A team interview is the two-on-one interview, in which two interviewers handle one applicant simultaneously. Most often, team interviewing is used with applicants for technical types of jobs in cases where the employment interviewer doesn't know much about the technical aspects of the work. In this case, the department head or perhaps a research person is brought in to participate in the interview along with the employment representative. Typical justifications are that this approach saves time, as compared with having the same two individuals interview the applicant sequentially, and that the possibility of repeating questions is eliminated.

Although these points are debatable, there are many drawbacks to the team approach to interviewing. Taken together, they greatly decrease the chance that a good line of communication will be established.

Whenever the number of people increases, the communication problems concommitantly increase manyfold. This is true of communication in most instances but is especially applicable to communication in the interview situation, where the presence of an extra person creates additional stress on the applicant. If the candidate is a relatively unsophisticated person or if she is not particularly interview-wary, the two-on-one situation can be very difficult to handle. It takes a very experienced interviewer to develop a rapport in a team situation. Many such interviews end up strictly as an interrogation in which the two interviewers seem to "gang up" on the poor outnumbered applicant. Needless to say, this turns out to be very uncomfortable and unprofitable for all the parties involved.

In addition, many team interviews fail to provide the applicant with the opportunity to ask enough questions to satisfy his or her own needs. Since a major philosophy of the interview is that it should allow both parties—the candidate as well as the interviewer—to meet their needs, this lack of questioning time on the part of the applicant is another drawback to the team interview.

For those who still believe the advantages of the team interview outweigh the disadvantages and who intend to continue using this approach, some recommendations follow.

Designate one team member as the person who will manage the interview. This key team member should control the course of the interview. Normally, this would be the interviewer from the personnel department, rather than his or her counterpart from the technical division.

Establish some meeting of the minds prior to the interview, to establish objectives for each of the interviewers. As much as possible, attempt to reduce the interview to a one-on-one situation or rather, a series of one-on-one situations. For example, the first interviewer might cover certain topics and objectives during the first 10 or 15 minutes, while the other party listens quietly. Then, after the first interviewer completes his cones to cover his objectives, the second interviewer has a similar amount of time to ask questions in his or her area of expertise. If one interviewer is from personnel, he will usually explore the more subjective areas—the applicant's attitudes and feelings, his energy level, his general educational background, and so forth. Then, assuming that the second interviewer is a technical resource person, he will address his questions toward the applicant's technical education, his precise knowledge of the technical aspects of the job, and so on. This creates a one-on-one situation during each phase of the interview, so that the candidate knows who is covering what and can establish a relationship with each interviewer consecutively. Chances for good communication are much better than in situations where interviewers fire questions alternately at the candidate.

After each interviewer has had his 10 or 15 minutes with the candidate, each should take an additional minute or two to ask any other questions he may desire to clear up, but here, too, the one-on-one situation should prevail. Then the candidate should be given ample time to ask any questions he may have about the job or about the company.

If a team is being used to train an interviewer or to expose a department head, for example, to the kinds of professional interviewing techniques that the personnel department has learned, it should be recognized as only a short-term instructional arrangement. The person being trained should be removed from the team and sent out to interview on her own just as soon as she feels comfortable in the interview environment.

In summary, those who intend to use team interviewing must have definite plans and objectives for the interview and must recognize the limitations and problems of the team interview. Whenever possible, try to stay away from the team interview, because it can be a very difficult situation in which to establish a good rapport.

BOARD INTERVIEWS

The board interview is one in which three or more interviewers face one applicant simultaneously. This approach has been a tool of the civil service for generations, both in state and federal government agencies in the U.S. and in many nations and provinces overseas. Board interviews are also frequently used in large companies to select management trainees. The typical reason given in support of board interviewing is that this procedure enables quite a few people to view and question the candidate at one time. This not only saves time, it is argued, but also takes into account various political considerations in many cases. The board interview is also frequently advocated because—especially in the case of a politically sensitive candidate who is being considered for a government position—nobody knows who voted for or against the candidate. Thus it is convenient for "buck-passing." It also allows rapid screening of large numbers of candidates, proponents claim, and it eliminates redundancy.

Despite these arguments for the board interview, it is an undesirable situation and should be discouraged. Its problems are the same as those inherent in the team approach but magnified manyfold. If it is difficult to develop a good line of communication in a one-on-one situation and even more difficult in two-on-one interviews, it is virtually impossible once the difficulties are compounded by having five or six persons interrogating one applicant. Very few candidates, if they are at all sensitive, are going to bare their souls by talking about highly personal feelings or experiences in front of five or six strangers. They're much more likely to do so in a one-on-one situation under private and confidential circumstances with an interviewer with whom they have had an opportunity to establish a rapport.

Nevertheless, many interviewers are forced, either by their company's decree or by the laws of their state, province, or nation, to participate in board interviews. There are a few tips that can help maximize the effectiveness of the board approach if it must be utilized.

First, it is imperative to have a chairperson of the interviewing board—one who really understands the interviewing process and who has prepared for the interview and forced the other board members to prepare. Each board member should study the job needs and the applicant's background prior to the interview; each should have an objective and a time sequence in which he or she can pursue that objective while the other board members are listening quietly. Only a skilled chairperson who recognizes the limitations of the board interview can effectively orchestrate this whole procedure, keep the participants on the track, and manage the flow of the interview.

A slightly different form of the board interview may be effective under limited circumstances. This variety involves a candidate who is required to be expert in a narrow discipline—say, one of the sciences. Before a board of 5–10 experts, the candidate first makes a formal presentation without interruption. Then the observers ask him questions designed to sample his knowledge in the particular area of the discipline with which they are most familiar. This sort of two-phase board approach resembles the oral examinations given by some universities to doctoral candidates. In those few instances in which the candidate is expected to know enough about the job to make a presentation pertinent to the job needs, it can be a good way of determining the depth of his job-related knowledge, but it is an ineffective way of evaluating his work-related attitudes and feelings.

In either type of board interview, preparation prior to the actual interview is essential. In selecting objectives for each board member to accomplish, it is also imperative that each member be held responsible for evaluating those objectives that have been established for him. Since each member will presumably inquire into the areas in which he or she has special expertise, it stands to reason that each should then be held responsible for the evaluation of the candidate in these areas along with the formation of a general impression of the candidate. It is up to the chairperson to hold each member to these responsibilities and to a subsequent explanation to the rest of the board as to the basis for his or her evaluation. This is especially important where technical areas are involved and where persons unfamiliar with this particular area will be expected to vote either for or against the candidate.

The board interview, like the team interview, should progress in series of one-on-one situations. Only when the climate becomes particularly intense should the chairperson interrupt and put it back on the right track. Just as in the team interview, each board member should have an opportunity for additional questions at the end of the interview, and the applicant should also have the chance to ask questions of the board. The applicant's questions should be handled by the board chairperson, who can either answer them personally or, if necessary, refer them to the appropriate board member.

HIRING-DECISION INTERVIEWS

Although the hiring-decision interview is actually a form of the in-depth interview, it merits special mention here because of a few important differences. In most instances, the hiring-decision interview will be the final step in a series of interviews. Except in the case of unskilled employees, perhaps, most companies and organizations today do not invest any one employee with the authority to screen, interview, and hire personnel without input from others within the organization. For a professional, technical, or managerial employee, at least three interviews—a screening interview, an in-depth interview, and a hiring-decision interview—are common practice. Whereas the first two interviews in this series may be conducted by a professional interviewer from the personnel or employment division of the organization, the final, or hiring-decision, interview will almost always be the responsibility of the manager under whom the candidate will work.

If the personnel who conducted earlier interviews have done their jobs thoroughly, they will have investigated many of the attitudes and subjective characteristics desirable for the job. However, especially if they are employment or personnel experts, they will have limited ability to evaluate the candidate's technical background and qualifications. This aspect of the investigation, then, must fall to the manager, and this should be the primary focus of the hiring-decision interview.

The manager will want to plan his cones to get at these technical areas. If the candidate has advanced degrees in such areas as accounting, computer programming, engineering, or one of the sciences, that should be the manager's target of concentration when he explores the educational area. In exploring past employment, he should similarly concentrate in depth on technical aspects of the job. Exactly what did this candidate do, step by step? What kinds of projects has he worked on? What was the subject of his thesis? What actual tasks has he been called upon to perform in the field, and what sorts of skills and knowledge has he brought to bear upon these tasks?

Many managers like to explore the depth of a candidate's technical knowledge by posing hypothetical problems or situations during the hiring-decision interview and then asking the applicant what steps he would take to solve or handle these problems. Such "hypotheticals" are a good way of determining the degree of flexibility the applicant has in applying his background and training to new situations.

If a candidate has always worked on projects or teams, it is important during the hiring-decision interview to isolate the person from the project and to determine specifically what his individual contribution was. Many scientists and engineers who work on projects are hung up on what "we" did, and their own personal expertise cannot be determined until they are isolated from the other persons on the project.

The manager may also want to obtain references from the interviewee—persons with specific knowledge of the applicant's expertise in the technical area, as opposed to general character references. These might include former professors in the major subject area, project managers, and so forth, who could supply specific details about the candidate's technical skills, knowledge, and experience.

In summary, then, the hiring-decision interview should focus on technical requirements for the job. The manager should concentrate primarily on these areas which no other interviewer in the company can evaluate as well as she can. Of course, this does not mean that she should completely ignore indicators of important attitudes and subjective characteristics, but she should not seek them at this stage in the employment process to the exclusion of the technical qualifications. At the close of the hiring-decision interview, the manager should be able to combine what she has learned with the prior evaluations of other interviewers to reach a decision. She should know exactly which candidate she wants to hire and why she wants that particular one, and she should be able to rank the others in order of preference, based on very solid reasons, in case her first choice decides not to accept the job offer. If the manager does not know at the end of the hiring interview whether she wants the candidate or not, then the entire interview has missed the mark because no intelligent hiring decision has been made possible.

Index

8 4 9 8 7 6 5 4